Evolving Partnerships

Evolving Partnerships

A Guide to Working with Business for Greater Social Change

JEM BENDELL

Jem Bendell of Lifeworth Consulting in Switzerland wrote this guidebook, with support from Griffith Business School's Asia Pacific Centre for Sustainable Enterprise (APCSE). The author can be contacted via www.lifeworth.com/consult and APCSE via www.griffith.edu.au/business/sustainable-enterprise.

Published by Greenleaf Publishing Limited
Aizlewood's Mill
Nursery Street
Sheffield S3 8GG
UK
www.greenleaf-publishing.com

Printed in Great Britain on acid-free paper by
Antony Rowe Ltd, Chippenham and Eastbourne.

FSC
www.fsc.org
MIX
Paper from
responsible sources
FSC® C013604

Cover by LaliAbril.com

British Library Cataloguing in Publication Data:
    Bendell, Jem.
        A guide to working with business for greater social change.
        -- (Evolving partnerships ; v. 1)
        1. Strategic alliances (Business) 2. Partnership. 3. Social
        responsibility of business. 4. Industries--Social aspects.
        5. Sustainable development.
        I. Title II. Series
        658.4'08-dc22

ISBN-13: 9781906093624 (hardback)
ISBN-13: 9781907643170 (PDF eBook)

Contents

Foreword

Business is everywhere, markets are all-pervasive and some companies are so large they bestride the planet with ease, dwarfing many national economies. Coming to terms with this reality requires public-interest organisations, such as charities, associations and United Nations agencies, to be more innovative, creative and strategic in the way they go about their work – if they are to be successful. All government involves the state and business working together, sometimes in open partnership and sometimes in less transparent collaboration. In many countries civil society is also an active and open part of the governance equation and is seen as viable, useful, knowledgeable and accountable. Understanding the relationship between these three aspects of society – government, business and civil society – has been at the heart of much of Jem Bendell's path-breaking partnership work over the last decade and more.

Given the realisation that it is important to understand the power of business and these new social partnerships, it would be remiss of any organisation tasked with promoting positive social change or well-being not to explore how it can better engage business organisations to deliver on its mandate. That realisation has been shared by many in the not-for-profit and intergovernmental sectors for some years. Indeed, a decade ago, many such organisations were preparing for an international summit in South Africa that would promote and officially recognise partnerships between themselves and businesses. In 2002 the World Summit for Sustainable Development marked the coming of age of cross-sectoral collaborations for sustainable development, with over 200 partnerships being announced and applauded by member states of the UN. Since then there has been a proliferation of partnerships around the world, addressing diverse issues from climate change to cancer research, and from malnutrition to malaria. A great deal of hope was demonstrated in this apparent teaming up on various challenges. Given this growth, it is important to take stock of what such partnerships are achieving, and how they can be improved.

Evolving Partnerships shows how voluntary cross-sectoral collaborations can achieve remarkable results, but are often limited in the extent to which they can address what are often interconnected global challenges. Collaborations on responsible forest certification, for instance, have led to large swathes of forest certification, yet have not curbed rates of tropical deforestation worldwide, as the market for irresponsibly sourced timber and pulp still exists. How partnerships in responsible forestry can repurpose some of their skills, resources and networks to influence those unconscious markets for timber and pulp as well as promoting intergovernmental cooperation on forest conservation will be key to the future health of the world's forests – the planet's lungs – and therefore ourselves.

That growing awareness is important because the challenge of creating a fair and sustainable global society requires engaging with the complex systems that constitute our world. Paul Cilliers has noted how:

> Each element of a complex system is ignorant of the behaviour of the system as a whole, it responds only to information that is available to it locally . . . If each element 'knew' what was happening to the system as a whole, all of the complexity would be present in that element . . . Complexity is the result of a rich interaction of simple elements that only respond to the limited information each of them are presented with.

The implication is that we need to connect in order to grow our understanding, and through connection become part of a network of knowledge and action.

The challenge, and the opportunity, for all organisations, is to shift to more systemic thinking, and find ways to apply that in our organisational strategies and work programmes. We are at a moment where, according to Thomas Kuhn's definition of a paradigm shift, 'one conceptual world-view is replaced by another'. Kuhn argued that scientific advancement is not evolutionary, but rather is a 'series of peaceful interludes punctuated by intellectually violent revolutions'. We are at such a moment, where people are increasingly appreciating society as systems of interaction, and the need to change the relations between people and organisations in order to achieve lasting change. Cross-sectoral partnerships are crucibles for this new way of thinking, as participants are exposed to the very different assumptions, aims and priorities that exist in different sectors of business, government and civil society. A good partner is one who begins to appreciate a wider reality than that first envisaged.

A new organisational species is emerging from the fertile interactions of business, not-for-profits and government agencies. These partnership organisations can themselves evolve, as the participants learn about the potential and limits of their collaboration. Strong cross-sectoral partnerships will not remain static in their mission and action, but evolve to address broader and deeper challenges of our time. As Charles Darwin wrote, 'it is not the strongest of the species that survives, nor the most intelligent; it is the one most adaptable to change'. This book by Jem Bendell, the pioneer of cross-sectoral partnering for sustainable development, shows why partnerships must evolve, how some are doing that, and provides tools to help evolve your own partnering for greater social impact. If you are considering how to engage business for greater impact, then this book is a timely guide.

Professor Malcolm McIntosh
Asia Pacific Centre for Sustainable Enterprise
Griffith University,
Queensland, Australia
December 2010

Acknowledgements

I thank David F. Murphy for discussing the various ideas in this guide, trialling some of the exercises with NGOs, and commenting on early drafts. Malcolm McIntosh at Griffith Business School's Asia Pacific Centre for Sustainable Enterprise supported the publication. Kate Ives at AccountAbility and Tim Bishop at CARE International UK trialled the workshop tools and provided feedback on the guidebook. I also thank Janna Greve for research assistance and Lala Rimando for text editing, and I thank Ian Doyle and Tapan Sarker for research assistance on the issue of partnerships for economic development. Tom Davies and Peter Utting have been key to my development of a critically constructive approach to corporate responsibility collaborations, and the late Jill Bowling provided me with the opportunity to reconnect with NGO strategies and practices in this field, which helped me understand the need for greater support for public-interest organisations in their private-sector relations.

Introduction

For those of us working on matters of public interest, whether social, environmental or cultural concerns, the extent of business and finance today is impossible to ignore. Private enterprise is fundamental not only to our economies, but also our culture, society and politics. Whatever social or environmental issue is considered today, a corporation or bank is involved in some way, either participating in a problem, providing solutions, or shaping what are considered viable options for addressing the problem. If we compare annual national gross domestic product (GDP) and company annual turnover, in 2009, of the largest 150 economies on our planet, 91 were corporations, not countries. Forty-six companies comprise the largest 100 economies in our world, with Walmart larger than Sweden or Saudi Arabia, and Exxon Mobil larger than Denmark or South Africa. Royal Dutch Shell is larger than Morocco, Vietnam and Slovakia combined (see **Box 1**).[1] The size of corporations serves to remind us that most, if not all, of the issues we work on in the fields of environmental or social progress are symptoms of deeper themes, which are shaped by economic rules and actors. If we are concerned with deforestation, it is not possible to have a significant scalable impact through

---

1   These figures were prepared by integrating a list of the 100 largest countries by GDP in 2009, from the International Monetary Fund, with a list of the 100 largest companies by turnover, which was crowd-sourced by contributors to Wikipedia. The comparison is valid due to GDP and turnover both being financial measures of total throughput. Sources: International Monetary Fund, *World Economic Outlook Database, October 2010: Nominal GDP List of Countries* and en.wikipedia.org/wiki/List_of_companies_by_revenue.

lobbying for the establishment of national parks or the purchase of land to conserve. Rather, the economic systems that drive forest conversion into agriculture and plantations must be addressed. If we are working on reducing rural poverty in India, our impacts will be limited if we do not work on why people are not able to generate greater surplus from their economic activities in order to afford insurance, health care, schooling and so forth. Given that realisation of the importance of economic factors in social and environmental situations, it is not possible to be effective in social change if we do not have a strategic approach for engaging the private sector.

The urgency of our work can easily be forgotten amid the day-to-day machinations of office politics and a demanding inbox. It is important to remember then that the vital signs of our world call for us to redouble our efforts, to be courageous and challenging, both within and outside our organisations. In the last 24 hours, 80,000 acres of tropical rainforest have been lost.[2] In a day, over a million tonnes of toxic waste have been released into our environment.[3] In just the last 24 hours, 98,000 people on our planet died of starvation, tens of thousands of them children.[4] In just this last day, over 150 species have been driven into extinction.[5] These problems exist, not because people have ignored them – many of us have been engaged for a long time, and generations before us. There is a need for new approaches that strike at the root of the problems. Looking again at the role of business and finance in causing the problems and potentially offering the solutions must be part of this more systemic approach.

If we are to achieve the massive changes in economy and society to address the myriad global challenges we face, we will need business professionals to be active members of a social movement to transform economies. As an activist, I have protested in the past, with the mobilisation around the G8 Summit in Genoa in 2001 being a particularly memorable experience. However, from what I know of the machines of business, government and intergovernmental bodies, it is clear to me that no amount of marches, vigils,

2   *The Guardian*, 'Protect nature for world economic security, warns UN biodiversity chief', 16 August 2010; www.guardian.co.uk/environment/2010/aug/16/nature-economic-security.

3   Data recalculated from GRID-Arendal, 'Vital Waste Graphics', 2004; www.grida.no/publications/vg/waste.

4   Data recalculated from United Nations Information Service, Independent Expert On Effects Of Structural Adjustment, Special Rapporteur On Right To Food Present Reports: Commission Continues General Debate On Economic, Social And Cultural Rights. United Nations, 29 March 2004.

5   Data recalculated from news.minnesota.publicradio.org/features/2005/01/31_olsond_biodiversity and www.rain-tree.com/facts.htm.

songs, videos or emails from individuals will of themselves shift attitudes. Instead, these actions must be complemented by people taking risks in their professional lives. Outsider activism can raise an issue on an agenda, but it does not shape the policy response, and it is at that moment of developing policy that the effectiveness, efficiency and fairness of an intervention is determined. For this reason I believe it is crucial that more people start to think and act as a 'corporate responsibility movement', which I explored in some depth in my last book.[6]

There are long traditions of civil-society engagement with business and finance, but a new era is called for. Trade unions have a long history of both conflict and collaboration with firms. Political movements have also engaged companies, such as during colonial times, when corporations were the sub-contractors of imperial powers, and thus the focus of anticolonial leaders. Of more recent origin, non-governmental organisations (NGOs) have been confronting corporations for decades. One of the most famous examples, due to extensive media coverage in the mid 1990s, was the environmental group Greenpeace's occupation of the Brent Spar oil platform which the oil company Shell was planning to sink in the North Atlantic. In recent years Greenpeace has renewed its brand-bashing campaigns: for instance, targeting Swiss food giant Nestlé over its connection with tropical deforestation through the purchase of palm oil. Confrontation is one tactic, but collaboration can also be sought, to leverage the power of the private sector towards your public-interest goal.

Innovative collaboration for sustainable development was something I became interested in while at university, and on graduation in 1995 I immediately went to work for the environmental group WWF-UK. In the Forest Unit, I worked with a group of companies that had committed to sourcing all their wood and wood products from sustainably managed forests. The group was key to developing market demand for a certification system for sustainable forests, the Forest Stewardship Council (FSC). WWF had been pressuring governments to agree to do something about tropical deforestation for years, and had not seen much movement, and so along with other NGOs they had turned their attention to the companies that were buying the wood products from trashed forests. Some NGOs attacked the companies with protests and boycotts, and WWF positioned itself as a partner to help the companies ensure that their wood came from reputable sources. It

6   Jem Bendell (ed.), *The Corporate Responsibility Movement: Five Years of Global Corporate Responsibility Analysis from Lifeworth, 2001–2005* (Sheffield, UK: Greenleaf Publishing, 2009; www.greenleaf-publishing.com/crmovement).

was an open-plan office at WWF-UK, and the head of the WWF International Endangered Seas campaign sat next to me, and overheard the work we were doing. After a few lunches discussing ideas, he set me the task of exploring whether the same certification process could be applied to sustainable fisheries, and as a result I helped develop the concept for the Marine Stewardship Council (MSC). Today there are about 134,595,610 hectares of forests certified under the FSC framework, and 4,000 seafood products available with the MSC eco-label.

I considered these partnerships with companies to be an important new way for NGOs and other public-interest organisations to work, and so co-wrote a book about it with David F. Murphy, *In the Company of Partners*.[7] In that book we described such partnerships as uncommon alliances, which emerge out of conflict, to provide innovative solutions to sustainable development challenges. Writing over 13 years later, an internet search for 'cross-sector partnerships' generates more than 140,000 webpages, uncovering a range of partnerships and associated specialists, tools, news and views. This is testament to the way in which the intervening years have seen people around the world reaching across traditional organisational divides to find new ways of generating change. A 2009 tome on the subject reports that 'the importance and impact of corporate–NGO engagements – both adversarial and collaborative – is growing'.[8]

In the 15 years that I have worked with or advised NGOs and UN agencies on their relations with corporations, I have often met people who feel conflicted and confused about how to engage with business. Some staff have a limited understanding of companies and due to this would prefer to take their money and not ask too many questions. Others have a critical view of how companies operate and their involvement in causing many of the problems of the world, and they also do not want a deep engagement with companies, either ignoring them or taking their funds without involving them closely in projects. Other staff are primarily focused on fundraising, see the opportunity of new sources of funding, and are happy to throw open the doors of their organisation to corporate partners. It is fairly rare that I find people with a critical view of the economic causes of our myriad social and environmental challenges, yet with an interest in exploring how to work with some corporate executives in strategic alliances that can

7   David F. Murphy and Jem Bendell, *In the Company of Partners: Business, Environmental Groups and Sustainable Development Post-Rio* (Bristol, UK: The Policy Press, 1997).

8   Michael Yaziji and Jonathan Doh, *NGOs and Corporations: Conflict and Collaboration* (Cambridge, UK: Cambridge University Press, 2009).

create a wider change. It is to encourage that attitude, and to advise such people, that I have written this guidebook. Some commentators on cross-sector partnering have said that good partnerships are like good marriages, where you do not try to change your partner. However, this ignores the fact that the objective of partnering may be precisely to create a change in the corporate partner. Partnership is neither marriage nor compromise, but a strategic alliance with the purpose of creating change, learning and infecting one's ideas into other organisations and sectors. My aim is to help guide this process of influencing corporate partners for greater social change.

When considering how to equip one's organisation or programme with the necessary skills to engage companies in new ways, many leaders of NGOs or UN agencies hire staff from the private sector. Although such staff exchanges are important, it is not sufficient to rely on private-sector staff to develop and implement strategic forms of engagement. Rather, engaging business for social change is a specialism in itself, with many years of experience and analysis from which to draw. With this guidebook I seek to distil some of those lessons for strategic planning. In particular, the guidebook is intended for people who work within civil-society or public-sector organisations and who already partner with companies. I refer to such organisations as 'public-interest organisations', implying that they seek to represent a public interest or provide a public benefit.[9] There is a growing amount of partnering support for companies, such as reports for business on partnering with NGOs and UN agencies, and business advisory services.[10] However, public-interest organisations are not often provided with such support, particularly at an advanced, strategic level, and it is this gap that the guidebook seeks to address.

As the Western financial crisis generates a further retreat of the state from various areas of society, so new attention will be paid to business contributions to society, while public-interest organisations will need to find new sources of income, or ways of levering smaller resources for greater impact. As such, the attention of public-interest organisations on the private sector is likely to grow, making cross-sector partnerships a continuing feature of

---

9 I recognise that some may dispute whether some organisations in civil society and governmental sectors are either intending or delivering public benefit, and that some others may claim that for-profit enterprises can be founded with a public-benefit objective. However, I use this term to clarify that I intend this guide to provide support to public-interest organisations that work with business across sectors.

10 See for instance the *Business Guide to Partnering with NGOs and the United Nations* (Dalberg Global Development Advisors and UNGC, 2007).

collective action on public issues. Some governments, including the United States, now even regard partnerships as a dimension to their foreign policy, helping to promote international understanding.[11] Cross-sector partnering is likely to become more, not less, important in the years to come, in many parts of the world.

Although many new partnerships are being formed, and many new people exposed to partnership ways of working, the field of practice includes over 13 years of published analysis on what works and what does not. This period of partnering has led to remarkable successes, but it has also resulted in a range of concerns about effectiveness and accountability. There is the risk of a form of partnership ideology, or 'partnerism', where the existence of partnership is seen as important in itself, with limitations and conflicts managed away rather than addressed directly.[12] However, many partners have learned from what works, as well as the limitations of their efforts. Many now ask themselves how to achieve a greater scale of impact to match the magnitude of the social and environmental challenges they face. This guidebook is intended to help such partnership practitioners find answers and transform their work with business for greater social impact.

Although recent years have seen the growth of a professional practice in partnering, and the support of groups such as The Partnering Initiative,[13] much of the focus to date has been on operational issues, rather than on the strategic challenge of evolving partnerships to achieve a greater scale of impact. The Partnering Initiative notes how 'partnerships – even many of those operating at very grass roots levels – are increasingly seeking not just to expand their activities but also to expand their influence'.[14] Consequently there is a need for more guidance for partners seeking to achieve greater social change. Rather than helping you with *moving on* from partnerships, this guidebook is intended to help you with *moving up* to a greater scale of impact. Advanced partnership practitioners will therefore benefit from using this guidebook, which focuses on how partnerships can evolve to generate systemic change.

---

11 US State Department, *The Global Partnership Initiative* (2010; www.state.gov/s/partnerships).

12 See for instance Jem Bendell, Eva Collins and Juliet Roper, 'Beyond Partnerism: Toward a More Expansive Research Agenda on Multi-stakeholder Collaboration for Responsible Business', *Business Strategy and the Environment* 19.6 (September 2010): 351–99, and Maria May Seitanidi, *The Politics of Partnerships: A Critical Examination of Nonprofit-Business Partnerships* (Springer, 2010).

13 www.thepartneringinitiative.org

14 Eva Halper, *Moving On: Effective Management for Partnership Transitions, Transformations and Exits* (London: International Business Leaders Forum, 2009): 16.

This guidebook uses evolution as a frame for two reasons. First, evolution refers to a general notion of progress as people and organisations learn through interacting with their environments. In my years as partnership researcher, adviser and educator I have found that the aims of partnerships and their participants have evolved to address more systemic causes of the specific issues that concern the partners. Building on this experience, I outline in this guidebook three generations in the evolution of cross-sector partnering.

The second reason for employing evolution as a frame is because I draw insights from the latest biological evolutionary theory on how complex systems can sustain themselves over time, and translate this into a method for understanding and assessing partnering practice. In 2009, the 150th anniversary of the publication of Charles Darwin's *On the Origin of Species* promoted wider reflections on the state of evolutionary sciences and thinking in society, including by ourselves. Although the implications of biological evolution theories for understanding society have often been viewed in relation to competition, evolution can help us understand cooperation as well. Darwin himself argued that humans are biologically inclined to be sympathetic, altruistic and moral, as this proved to be an advantage in the struggle for existence.[15] In recent years the role of cooperation in evolution has become clearer, due to scientific interest in how the survival of an organism depends on the survival of groups of organisms, which depends on the survival of ecosystems as a whole.[16] As it is 150 years since biological evolution was clearly articulated by Darwin, this is an opportune time to explore how evolution can help us understand the increasing interconnections between people and organisations and the implications for progressive change, as recognised by some management academics.[17]

This guidebook provides a combination of commentary, boxes for clarification, and 11 exercises. It starts by outlining the role and nature of cross-sector partnerships today as a mechanism for public-interest organisations to further their organisational mandates. In so doing it describes the typical process of partnering, and how partners learn about the benefits and limits

---

15   Charles Darwin, *The Descent of Man* (London: Watts & Co., 1971, 1930): 141.

16   It is not implied here that Darwinian evolution is actually taking place at an organisational level, but that it is a useful metaphor and framework for thinking about interconnectedness, interdependence, competition and change. Therefore in this guide I am not seeking to contribute to the three areas of study that apply evolutionary concepts to society: evolutionary psychology, evolutionary theory in management, and memetics (see Box 18).

17   Jonathan Smith and John Rayment, 'Globally Fit Leadership: Four Steps Forward', *Journal of Global Responsibility* 1.1 (2010): 55–65.

of their partnerships and can thus evolve the focus of their work accordingly. In doing that it maps out three distinct generations of partnership, which are defined by the focus of their ambition. Examples are given of success and failure, where failure is largely due to the limits of individual corporate action, and therefore suggests a need for new forms of collaboration that address the systemic causes of the problems we seek to address. Throughout that flow of argumentation, exercises are provided to help you clarify your own perspectives on the matters at hand. A key aim for the exercises is to help you evolve your partnering to achieve a wider level of impact – a level that responds to the scale, depth and urgency of the challenges we face today. Before concluding, some of the emerging risks of system-change-oriented partnerships are outlined, with some recommendations for how to manage those risks. The increasingly important role of cross-sector partnering in promoting international development is examined, with advice given for what to look for in potential corporate partners in development work. Yet the conclusions are more personal than organisational, as the effectiveness of partnering depends on the mindfulness of managers in each organisation, to stay focused on the public goals, rather than the partnership, and to not confuse the two.

You can read the guidebook yourself without doing the exercises, or use it with your team and go through the exercises together. The exercises in this guidebook were trialled during a participatory evaluation and strategic planning workshop with CARE International, one of the top three charitable aid agencies committed to fighting poverty and injustice in 70 countries. If you would like to evaluate and re-plan your partnering during a facilitated workshop that incorporates these exercises, please contact Lifeworth Consulting (www.lifeworth.com/consult). Once you have read the book and completed the exercises you will be better prepared to begin more wide-ranging and creative conversations with your current and potential corporate partners. Then the real fun will begin. Rather than focusing on that aspect of cross-sector engagement, in this guidebook I seek to help you in achieving some strategic clarity about what you seek from your engagements with business.

If you are new to partnering, I recommend you read *The Partnering Toolbook*[18] before using this guidebook. If you work in the private sector, the guidebook may be useful for enhancing your understanding of the potential for public-interest organisations to evolve their strategic engagement with

18 Ros Tennyson, *The Partnering Toolbook* (The Partnering Initiative; London: International Business Leaders Forum, 2003)

companies. That is, of course, if they are paying any attention to the kind of advice shared in these pages!

Box 1 **The importance of business**

US$ millions in 2009 (GDP or corporate turnover)	Country or corporation
14,119,050	United States
5,068,894	Japan
4,984,731	People's Republic of China
3,338,675	Germany
2,656,378	France
2,178,856	United Kingdom
2,118,264	Italy
1,574,039	Brazil
1,467,889	Spain
1,336,066	Canada
1,236,943	India
1,231,892	Russia
994,246	Australia
874,810	Mexico
832,512	South Korea
796,651	Netherlands
614,466	Turkey
539,377	Indonesia
491,923	Switzerland
472,103	Belgium
430,736	Poland
413,800	Wal-Mart
406,072	Sweden
382,073	Austria
378,592	Norway
378,524	Republic of China (Taiwan)
376,268	Saudi Arabia
330,780	Greece
325,938	Iran
325,678	Venezuela
310,500	Exxon Mobil
310,093	Denmark
310,057	Argentina
287,219	South Africa
278,100	Royal Dutch Shell
263,979	Thailand
246,100	BP plc
238,607	Finland
233,478	Portugal
233,300	Saudi Aramco
232,403	Colombia
223,874	United Arab Emirates
222,156	Ireland
205,000	Toyota Motor Corporation
202,400	Sinopec
195,390	Israel
192,955	Malaysia
190,321	Czech Republic
187,954	Egypt
182,231	Singapore
173,400	Samsung Group
171,600	Chevron Corp.
168,843	Nigeria
164,390	ING Group
161,994	Pakistan
161,621	Chile
161,521	Romania
161,196	Philippines
156,700	General Electric
152,800	ConocoPhillips →

150,800	Volkswagen Group	103,500	Société Générale
149,100	PetroChina	102,700	Siemens AG
148,300	Total S.A.	101,600	Crédit Agricole
139,763	Algeria	101,600	National Iranian Oil Company
139,600	Allianz		
129,900	Assicurazioni Generali	100,300	HBOS
		98,416	Kuwait
129,540	Hungary	98,313	Qatar
129,200	AXA	98,000	Koch Industries
126,766	Peru	97,800	Aviva
123,200	Carrefour	96,400	Statoil
123,000	AT&T Inc.	96,200	Petróleos de Venezuela
121,200	Fortis		
120,900	Eni	95,800	IBM
120,900	Bank of America	95,800	E.ON
119,800	Honda	95,500	Nestlé
118,300	Ford Motor Company	95,500	Deutsche Bank
118,300	Berkshire Hathaway	95,300	Valero Energy
117,794	New Zealand	94,602	Bangladesh
117,404	Ukraine	93,500	Deutsche Post
117,000	UBS AG	93,164	Vietnam
116,400	JPMorgan Chase	93,000	McKesson Corporation
116,200	BNP Paribas		
113,100	Daimler AG	92,000	Deutsche Telekom
113,100	Hitachi, Ltd.	91,800	Petrobras
110,100	American International Group	91,700	Dexia
		91,600	Nippon Telegraph and Telephone
109,800	Hyundai Kia Automotive Group		
		91,374	Morocco
108,500	Royal Bank of Scotland	89,400	Cardinal Health
		88,300	Cargill
108,200	Nissan Motors	88,210	Slovakia
107,891	Kazakhstan	88,000	SK Group
107,800	Verizon	88,000	Goldman Sachs
107,700	Hewlett-Packard	86,200	Fiat
106,400	Glencore International	85,300	Morgan Stanley
		84,600	BASF
105,200	Arcelor Mittal	83,700	Credit Suisse
104,600	General Motors	83,600	Tesco
104,500	Pemex	82,500	BMW
104,300	LG Group	82,400	Telefónica

81,700	Citigroup		**76,300**	CVS Caremark
81,600	Electricité de France		**75,400**	UnitedHealth Group Incorporated
79,700	Procter & Gamble			
79,700	Barclays Bank		**75,200**	Nokia
79,000	HSBC		**74,700**	PSA Peugeot Citroën
79,000	Metro AG		**74,474**	Angola
77,400	Home Depot, Inc.		**73,800**	Altria Group
77,300	France Télécom		**73,700**	ThyssenKrupp
77,200	Matsushita Electric Industrial			

1 A planet of partnerships

By bringing together their respective competencies and resources for the greater good, people in governments, business, civil-society and multilateral agencies have been seeking innovative ways to respond to many of the key development challenges of our time: the impact of climate change; human security; the prevention, management and treatment of HIV/AIDS and other major diseases; the generation of new investment, entrepreneurship and employment; and financing for development. The appetite for partnerships appears strong. Over 90% of corporate executives responding to a World Economic Forum survey felt that future 'partnerships between business, government, and civil society would play either a major role or some role in addressing key development challenges'.[1] These forms of societal partnership are the focus of this guidebook (see **Box 2**).

One initiative in particular demonstrates the important role of these innovative relations with the private sector. In 1999 UN Secretary-General Kofi Annan called for a 'global compact' with the private sector to promote UN goals.[2] A year later the United Nations Global Compact (UNGC) was launched

---

1 World Economic Forum, *Partnering for Success: Business Perspectives on Multistakeholder Partnerships* (Geneva: WEF, 2005): 5.

2 United Nations, Press Release, SG/SM/6881, 'Secretary-General Proposes Global Compact on Human Rights, Labour, Environment', in address to World Economic Forum in Davos (1999; www.un.org/News/Press/docs/1999/19990201.sgsm6881.html).

Box 2 **Defining partnership**

One definition of partnership is the 'state of being a partner'. The dictionary refers to 'partner' as 'a person you are closely involved with in some way'. When described in the traditional context of business incorporation, the partner, according to the dictionary, can be 'one of the owners of a company'. In an organisation considered as a partnership, the 'partners' share ownership and liability.

Since the late 1980s the term 'partnership' has become more widely used in describing both relations between organisations (often from different sectors) and new forms of organisation beyond the traditional business partnership model. Therefore, a useful distinction can be made between an 'inter-organisational partnership' and a 'partnership organisation'.

An inter-organisational partnership is an arrangement between two or more separate organisations to pursue a common activity or interest where risks and benefits are shared. Such partnerships may or may not involve formal agreements or financial exchange. They can be based on legally binding contracts or purely voluntary arrangements. The partners may have different activities that could serve a common interest, or may agree to work together and undertake a set of activities for different interests.

Partnership organisations, on the other hand, can involve either partners from a single sector, such as companies engaged in strategic alliances with other companies, or from different sectors, which include traditionally distinct ones like government agencies, civil-society organisations and private-sector businesses. The latter's cross-sector approach is sometimes referred to as a public–private partnership or PPP. However, many PPPs are essentially service delivery contracts where public-sector bodies engage with private-sector partners for the delivery of certain services such as waste management.[a]

This guidebook focuses on cross-sector collaborations between the private sector and organisations in the public or civil sectors that explicitly address a matter of public interest. For coming from different parts of society and for aiming to address issues of concern to society at large, these partnerships are considered 'societal'. These 'societal partnerships' are collaborations between organisations in two or more societal sectors that commit to share resources, risks and rewards to achieve agreed objectives for improving society.   →

a It could be argued that as public funds are being used in PPPs they should also be assessed in terms of their broader societal contribution, and I return to this point below.

Examples of cross-sector societal partnerships include Benetton and the United Nations Volunteers Programme, for the 2001 International Year of Volunteers, and the World Bank-initiated Business as Partners for Development and the Public–Private Partnership 2000 for national disaster reduction in the United States. For the most part, such partnerships are time-limited, while others may evolve into a partnership organisation when a new organisation is created with its own board and secretariat. Examples include the Forest Stewardship Council and the Global Alliance to Improve Nutrition.

In this guidebook I describe three generations of cross-sector partnership to emphasise an evolving focus on the scale of a partnership's impact on a public-interest matter.

and ten years later it had reached over 6,000 businesses in 120 countries, many of whom collaborate on practical projects with the UN system, government development agencies and civil society. For example, Daimler-Chrysler in South Africa works with the German Development Agency GTZ to help address HIV/AIDS. The partnership helps the company reach not only its own workers, but their families and the community as well, through an HIV/AIDS prevention and care programme. Another example highlighted by the UNGC is the comprehensive labour agreement signed between the oil firm Statoil and the International Federation of Chemical, Energy, Mine and General Workers' Unions.[3] The agreement between the Norwegian oil firm and the trade union group covers 16,000 employees in 23 countries. Hundreds of other innovative collaborations are described on the UNGC's website and in the reports from their participant companies.[4] At the UNGC's Tenth Anniversary Summit in New York the emphasis was on working with business towards a 'tipping point' that would make business responsibility and sustainability the norm. Such a goal requires more than increasing the number of partners or partnerships; it will involve transforming those relations into catalysts of wider social change. This guidebook provides one tool for reaching 'the tipping point'.

Although I offer a definition of partnership, the concept of partnership means different things in both form and function to different people. To clarify your perspectives and those of your colleagues, try **Exercise A** on understanding partnerships (see **Box 3**).

---

3   www.icem.org/?id=107
4   www.unglobalcompact.org

Box 3 **Understanding partnerships (Exercise A)**

This four-part exercise helps you to consider the concept of partnership and the reasons for and against partnering.

1. Exploring the term

- Write down at least three words that describe something similar to a partnership or partner
- Ask a colleague to do the same
- If in a team, put your answers on sticky notes, then place them on a flipchart
- Discuss in the team or with a colleague how partnership can be understood

2. Intuitive understandings

- Complete the following sentences with whatever first comes into your mind:

  'The corporate partnership I am working on is . . .

  _____

  _____

  'Partnerships won't . . .

  _____

  _____

- If completing on your own, take a moment to reflect on the implications of your intuition on partnering for your work
- If in a team, you can discuss with a colleague what you both wrote and any insights from that, and then share with the whole team, to generate awareness of the feelings of the team towards partnership

3. Clarifying hopes and concerns

- Identify three benefits for your organisation from an actual or potential corporate partnership, and three limitations or problems with this corporate partnership

Pros	Cons
_____	_____
_____	_____
_____	_____

- Identify three benefits for a company in partnering with your organisation, and three limitations or problems with partnering with your organisation

Pros	Cons
_____	_____
_____	_____
_____	_____

- If completing this in a team, discuss with a colleague what you both wrote, and then share with the whole team, to see what similarities and differences there are. (If completing on your own, move on to the next point.)
- Review the partial list of benefits and limitations of cross-sector partnering described briefly in **Box 4**
- Are there cases where a benefit or limit you identified differs from those identified by a colleague, or those identified in **Box 4**?
- Concern with 'agenda creep', cited in **Box 4**, is one reason why some companies do not sign up to the UNGC as they think it may evolve into a more defined set of standards that could then have legal repercussions, in contract as well as tort law. On the other hand, others might consider that it is a benefit that partnerships evolve as they learn. Are there other benefits that could be limitations, or vice versa, from either **Box 4** or your own lists? What does this mean for partnership management?
- What might happen if participants in partnerships ignore limitations, whether they are widely recognised or not?

Although cross-sector partnerships hold considerable potential as a new organisational form for promoting sustainable development and other societal aims, partners from the different sectors recognise that there are considerable inherent risks. NGOs and UN agencies are concerned that partnerships with business could threaten their integrity and independence. Some business people fear that too much time and money spent on partnerships with not-for-profit partners might divert them from their primary aim as profit-making enterprises – to produce goods and services that benefit their owners and workers. Governments often raise important questions about the legitimacy, governance and accountability of cross-sector partnerships, particularly those that exclude or undermine public-sector interests. As this kind of partnership has become a more widely used mechanism for policy development and implementation, questions about their effectiveness and accountability become more important. For example, as a particularly high-profile partnership involving the foremost global rule-making body, the UNGC received criticism in its first decade for not initially ensuring transparency in the performance of its member companies and not requiring a certain level of performance in return for the advantages of associating with the United Nations.[5] A number of benefits and limitations of partnering that have been identified in the literature are illustrated in **Box 4**, although you may have identified more during **Exercise A** (**Box 3**).

Box 4 **Some illustrative benefits and limits of partnership**

Group	Reasons for	Reasons against
Public-interest organisations Civil-society groups, intergovernmental organisations and government agencies with a public purpose	Funding	Public criticism
	In-kind support	Subverting regulation
Business All forms of private-sector companies including finance	New knowledge	Time-consuming
	Influencing regulation	Attracting unwanted attention
Politicians Within government or in opposition, not directly involved in the partnership	Social harmony	New diverse political coalitions
	Smarter civil servants	Unclear outcomes and time frame
Intended beneficiaries People whom partners claim to be helping through their partnership	New avenues of influence	Variable accountabilities
	Scalable market-based solutions	Less coordinated interventions
Wider society The general public, not directly involved in the partnership	Innovation on public issues	Uncritical policy paradigm
	Participation opportunities	Undermining electoral process

5   Jem Bendell, 'Flags of Inconvenience? The Global Compact and the Future of the United Nations', in Malcolm McIntosh, Georg Kell and Sandra Waddock (eds.), *Learning To Talk* (Sheffield, UK: Greenleaf Publishing, 2004; www.greenleaf-publishing.com/lttalk.htm): 146-67.

Some criticisms of partnerships arise due to this being a new area of professional practice. The UNGC, for instance, developed its reporting requirements and processes for registering the activity of participant companies after a few years.[6] Efforts to professionalise work in this field, such as The Partnering Initiative (TPI), are therefore particularly important. A useful framework developed by TPI to guide best practice is the Partnering Cycle. It identifies four main phases in any partnership: scoping and building, managing and maintaining, reviewing and revising, and sustaining outcomes.[7] The Collective Leadership Institute (CLI) offers a similar framework.[8] However, both critics and reflective partners ask deeper questions of partnerships which might not be addressed through better planning, communications or evaluations. Given the scale and urgency of challenges such as climate change, economic instability, resource depletion and persistent poverty, are partnerships able to achieve sufficient change to warrant their growing role? The Partnering Initiative argues that due to:

> the limitations of 'business as usual', many corporations, governments and international agencies [are looking to] cross-sector partnerships ... to bring about system change in the way we organise ourselves as humanity to better address the global challenges of the 21st century.[9]

In light of the need to scale up the ambition of partnering to promote system change, this guidebook upgrades the fourth phase of partnering, so that partners are supported in 'sustaining and evolving' partnerships. Therefore rather than partners repeating a scoping of issues and objectives similar to that undertaken when their partnerships began, insights from social sciences can help structure conversations and reflections to identify new possibilities for more systemic impact.[10] This expanded focus on how to, in the CLI's words, 'take it to the next level',[11] is portrayed by 'the partnership helix' (**Diagram I**), where partners not only consider institutionalising their partnership or moving on, but also how to evolve it to a significantly greater

---

6   See www.one-report.com/cop for the latest.

7   thepartneringinitiative.org/what_is_partnering.jsp

8   CCI, 'Typical Phases in Partnerships', Lecture at SEED (2007); www.collective-leadership.com/123live-user-data/user_data/3829/public/DOKUMENTE/021007_Workshop_CapeTown_SC_new.pdf.

9   tpi.iblf.org/areas_of_work/System_Change.jsp

10 For a guide that provides insight into managing partnership exits, as well as how to plan for longer-term issues, including partnership exit, at an early stage of partnership development, see Eva Halper, *Moving On: Effective Management for Partnership Transitions, Transformations and Exits* (London: IBLF, 2009).

11 CCI, 'Typical Phases in Partnerships'

level of impact. This reflects the learning of partners, which often leads to an evolution in the focus of a partnership.

There are 15 stages in the partnership helix, which can be summarised as follows:

1. **Scoping**. Understanding the issues; collecting information; consulting with stakeholders and potential donors; creating a vision for the partnership

2. **Identifying**. Identifying partners and – if suitable – securing their participation; encouraging them to collaborate

3. **Building**. Partners build their relationship through defining goals, objectives and principles that are the basis for their partnership

4. **Planning**. Partners identify activities and outline a full work programme

5. **Structuring**. Partners create a structure for their partnership as it develops over time

6. **Mobilising**. Participants and supporters identify and raise cash and non-cash contributions

7. **Delivering**. When resources are secured and project details confirmed, the implementation starts, with a timetable for specific deliverables

8. **Measuring**. Monitoring and reporting on the partners' and the partnership's outputs and outcomes in relation to the aims

9. **Reviewing**. Assessing the impact of the partnership on partner organisations and the issues being addressed

10. **Revising**. Changing the partnership objectives, processes or participants, if necessary, in light of the reviewing

11a. **Institutionalising**. Creating new structures and mechanisms for the partnership to last

11b. **Scaling**. Bringing in new participants and resources to replicate the existing partnership's activities

12. **Moving on**. Agreeing conclusion and how to exit the partnership in suitable ways

13 **Evolving**. A deeper consideration of how to build on the partnership to create a new level of impact that addresses the systemic causes of the problems addressed

14 **Re-planning**. As a result of the evolving goals, new activities and work programmes are agreed

15 **Restructuring**. As a result of the evolving goals and partners, a new structure is created for the partnership

Diagram I **The partnership helix**[12]

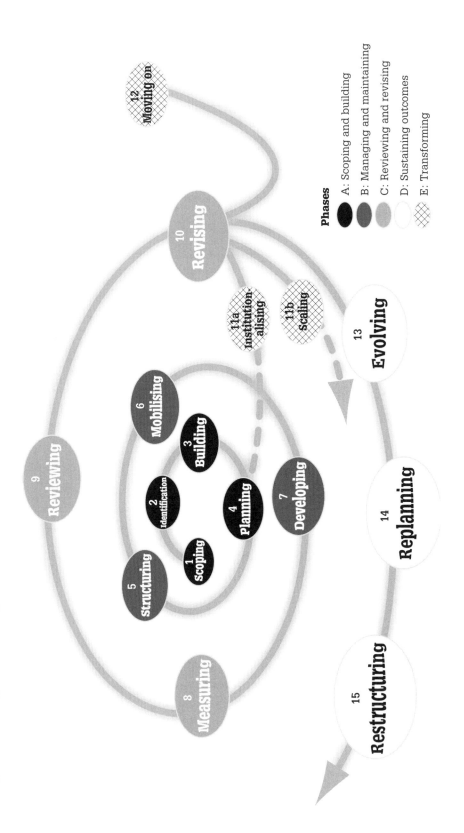

Phases

A: Scoping and building

B: Managing and maintaining

C: Reviewing and revising

D: Sustaining outcomes

E: Transforming

12 The Partnering Cycle is the copyright of IBLF. See Ros Tennyson, *The Partnering Toolbook* (The Partnering Initiative; London: International Business Leaders Forum, 2003).

2 Generations of partnership

A key advantage of partnerships, often cited by practitioners and analysts, is enhanced personal and organisational learning for all participants. The engagement with professionals working in other sectors enables people to expand their view on a particular challenge, and understand the relationships and interests that shape the situation.

Key to learning is being able to appreciate the limits of one's actions and ideas. This guidebook is based on that premise: for partnering to be a successful strategy for social change, it must evolve by addressing drawbacks and limitations. Exercise A may have highlighted some of these challenges with partnering. It may have also revealed the constant presence of paradox, as most positive aspects of partnering appear to have an associated negative. The degree of paradox depends on one's opinion and how wide one's view is cast on the 'knock-on' effects of a particular partnership. For instance, the 'wider society' benefits and drawbacks when 'innovation on public issues' is counterpoised by 'uncritical policy paradigm', or when 'participation opportunities' is counterpoised by 'undermining electoral process'. These debates were experienced by the UNGC coordinators, who had to balance the benefits from encouraging voluntarily responsible business with concerns about how some large companies were gaining unfair access to public policy processes and budget support from governments and developmental agencies.[1]

Paradox also may have emerged from the sentence completion tests in Exercise A, as many professionals feel ambiguous about what partnerships may or may not be achieving. The implication of this insight is that partnering is not in itself either good or bad, but that the usefulness of partnerships requires continual attention by the involved practitioners to the public goals, wider systems and personal intentions at play. If practitioners do not recognise, or choose to ignore, the limits of partnering, this not only restricts learning but also reduces the attention they give to goals, systems and intentions. If this happens, partnering may move from a useful methodology to an unhelpful ideology.

So what has been learned through over a decade of cross-sector partnering? A key learning is that the new relationships created across organisational divides can be the greatest strength, particularly if refocused for changing circumstances. According to TIP,

> The most successful and productive partnerships are those that do not resist change by trying to contain the partnership in a fixed format but rather accept, manage and even thrive on change as a key element in their partnering approach.[2]

For instance, partners may have come together to build a school but then decide that they need to work on rural livelihoods or the teacher training system in order to make schooling available. This relates to another key learning: that partnerships need to work at more macro levels in order to sustain progress at the local level to address the root causes of problems. Therefore, three stages or generations of partnering can be observed:

- First-generation partnerships involve a financial contribution from a business to a public-interest organisation, with some sharing of benefit, but little risk to the business, and little commitment beyond the financial donation

- Second-generation partnerships involve partners committing to change their internal operations in line with the objectives of the public-interest organisation. Sometimes financial contributions are

---

1   Ann Zammit, *Development at Risk: Rethinking UN–Business Partnerships* (Geneva: UN Research Institute for Social Development [UNRISD] and the South Centre, 2003).

2   Eva Halper, *Moving On: Effective Management for Partnership Transitions, Transformations and Exits* (London: IBLF, 2009): 19.

involved. The main focus is often on the operations of corporate partners

- Third-generation partnerships involve partners seeking to change their external operating contexts – sector, markets and societies – in order for them to be better supported to achieve internal changes for public goals, and to encourage non-partners to do the same

These generations are illustrated in **Diagram II**. The focus of first-generation partnerships is exclusively external, the second generation is primarily internal, and the third generation both, but linked. In the remainder of this section I provide some examples of partnerships in each of these generations, their benefits and limitations, and provide you an opportunity to assess the generation of your own partnerships.

Diagram II **The generations of partnership**

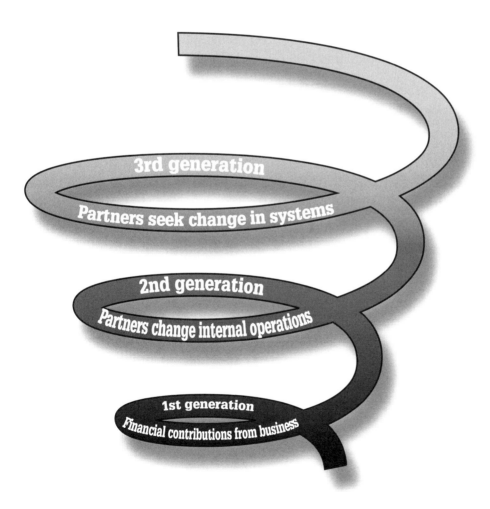

3rd generation
Partners seek change in systems

2nd generation
Partners change internal operations

1st generation
Financial contributions from business

First-generation partnerships are numerous, and this is the most typical form of collaborative relationship. The winners of the Asian CSR Awards in 2008 reflected the predominance of these forms of finance-based, cross-sector relationship in Asia, with all categories except for the workplace award acknowledging a firm's financial or in-kind support to projects external to the company.[3] For example, Johnson & Johnson received an award within the 'concern for health' category for their project in the Philippines to combat worm infection among school children. Launched in October 2007, 'War on Worms in Western Visayas' (WOW-V) is a two-year collaborative effort between Johnson & Johnson, the University of the Philippines in Manila, the Department of Health, the Department of Education and local-government units. The project maps the prevalence of worm infection and administers anthelmintic tablets twice a year to 300,000 children in government schools. The goal is to reduce cumulative prevalence of the soil-transmitted helminth worm by 50%, and heavy infections to near 0%, and thereby reduce rates of malnutrition and absenteeism, improving academic performance of public school children. The project is supported by Johnson & Johnson's donation of the tablets and by funding from the J & J Asia Pacific Contributions Committee and J & J Philippines Contribution Committee, together with resources from the counterpart organisations. The programme also involves meetings to encourage local governments to commit to provide drugs for its maintenance beyond two years and to address the sanitary concerns that are associated with worm infestation.[4]

Some do not consider that these forms of relationship warrant the term 'partnership', given that the transaction is almost exclusively one-way by means of financial or in-kind donations. I include them here as the term 'partnership' is often used by participants in such sponsorship relationships, and because they can often lead to more evolved forms of engagement. One example of how a sponsorship relationship can evolve into a closer collaboration is provided by the bank HSBC and the environmental WWF. Their association started in 1985, when HSBC sponsored the creation of the Centre for Environmental Technology. In 2002 the bank committed to contribute US$50 million over five years, to WWF, the Botanic Gardens Conservation International and Earthwatch. This 'Investing in Nature' partnership aimed

---

3 COMTEX, 'Announced – Asia's Foremost CSR Awards Programme' (Singapore: ACN Newswire via COMTEX, 22 November 2008; www.marketwatch.com/news/story/winners-asian-csr-awards-2008/story.aspx?guid=%7BC1C057B8-F992-4820-AD1A 8E7E0DE7F9D8%7D&newsid=944383666&&dist=bigchartssymb=INTC&sid=2564).

4 www.us-asean.org/cr/JJ_WOW-V.asp

to protect 20,000 plant species from extinction, conserve some of the world's major rivers, and send scientists and HSBC fieldworkers around the world to work on conservation. Although the species target was difficult to measure, 'globally, an area of 2.2 million hectares of land was managed, protected or restored through WWF's Investing in Nature freshwater programme' as a result of the partnership.[5]

The collaboration deepened as WWF encouraged HSBC to mainstream sustainability thinking into the bank's various business operations.[6] Therefore in 2003 HSBC adopted the Equator Principles, which address the environmental and social issues that arise in financing projects. In 2004 WWF-UK's head of conservation, Francis Sullivan, joined the HSBC staff as an environmental adviser.[7] By the end of that year HSBC had announced a commitment to becoming 'carbon-neutral' in its internal operations, which it announced it had achieved the following year, through reducing energy use, buying green electricity and purchasing of 'carbon offsets'.[8] At the end of the partnership, important motivational and skills outcomes were reported by HSBC staff,[9] and the bank doubled its commitment to the NGOs with the HSBC Climate Partnership in 2007.[10]

As **Box 5** indicates, there are a variety of benefits for all participants arising from first-generation partnerships. The main benefit for the public-interest organisation is a new source of finance and increased public profile. Cause-related marketing partnerships are particularly useful in this regard. Perhaps the most famous contemporary example is Product(RED), which generates funds from the sale of participating brands for the Global Fund Against Aids, TB and Malaria. **Box 6** outlines some the issues that a partnership like this entails, including some of the controversies that have arisen now that the initiative has grown significantly. This case study includes an exercise that you can do on your own or with colleagues.

---

5   WWF, 'HSBC & WWF' (2010; wwf.panda.org/what_we_do/how_we_work/
    businesses/corporate_support/business_partners/cp_hsbc).
6   www.wwf.org.uk/what_we_do/about_us/history/index.cfm
7   www.hsbc.com/1/2/newsroom/news/news-archive-2003/hsbc-appoints-
    environmental-adviser#top
8   www.hsbc.com/1/2/newsroom/news/news-archive-2005/hsbc-goes-carbon-
    neutral-three-months-early
9   Earthwatch, 'An Independent Report' (2007; www.earthwatch.org/europe/
    get_involved/involved_corporate/employee_engagement/engagement_why/
    cpi_evaluation).
10 www.earthwatch.org/europe/downloads/Our_Work/Earthwatch_HSBC_
    Climate_Partnership_Research_brief.pdf

Box 5 **Some illustrative benefits and limits of first-generation partnerships**

Group	Benefits	Limits
Public-interest organisations Civil-society groups, intergovernmental organisations and government agencies with a public purpose	Funding	Not changing the company
	Profile	Consumer confusion or public distrust
Business All forms of private-sector companies including finance	Marketing	Not learning from partners
	Public Relations	Distance from the beneficiaries
Politicians Within government or in opposition, not directly involved in the partnership	Greater charitable spending	Corporate influence on social programmes
	Increasing public awareness	Consumer confusion or distrust
Intended beneficiaries People whom partners claim to be helping through their partnership	Increased spending	Variable accountabilities
	Increased public awareness	Less coordinated interventions
Wider society The general public, not directly involved in the partnership	New opportunities to help	Confusion over product or firm contribution to the issue
	Greater business aspiration to benefit society	Commercialisation of needs

Organisations involved in research, which needs to be independent of commercial interests in order to be valid, face difficult issues with such forms of partnership. Public criticisms of corporate funding of studies influencing health regulation (such as the fielding of experts during a 2004 consultation on sugar's impact on health at the Food and Agriculture Organization) and studies on responsible business (such as British American Tobacco's financial support of the International Centre for CSR at the University of Nottingham, UK) have highlighted this problem in the past.[11] One response to these concerns is to seek greater distance, rather than proximity and exchange, between the public-interest organisation's work programme and the corpo-

---

11   See BBC, 'UN Probes Sugar Industry Claims', 8 October 2004; news.bbc.co.uk/2/ hi/health/3726510.stm, and *BMJ*, 'Row Over Nottingham Tobacco Cash Deepens', *BMJ* 322.1270 (2001); www.bmj.com/cgi/content/full/322/7297/1270/b.

rate donor. However, good conflict-of-interest management and partnership governance systems to ensure that key strategic decisions are not made by people dependent on continued corporate financing can be effective in addressing these issues.

There are many disadvantages if public-interest organisations fail to engage corporations more closely and critically. First, because the company, through their normal business operations, may have an effect on the intended beneficiaries or intended goal of the partnership. Not engaging on these issues is a missed opportunity. Second, external audiences, whether consumers witnessing the co-branding on products, or policy makers and opinion formers seeing co-branding in published literature, typically view the relationship as a complete one, implying the organisation is generally responsible. Therefore, the general public may assume that buying a product or service from the involved company would make a net positive contribution to the issue concerned. For instance, a person buying a Product(RED) mobile phone from Motorola may think they are making a positive contribution to the struggle with HIV/AIDS. Likewise, a policy maker reading a publication from an AIDS charity supported by Motorola might think the company provides a net positive contribution to addressing the disease. In addition, some may derive an impression about the company beyond the issue of HIV/AIDS, and consider that Motorola is making a positive contribution to public health. None of these impressions would necessarily be false, but neither would they necessarily be true (See **Box 6**). Such partnerships need to ensure that there is greater clarity and transparency about the partners' roles and contributions. A third disadvantage of not addressing the social or environmental performance of the corporate partner presents itself if the public-interest organisation is a governmental development ministry, such as USAID or GTZ. If their corporate partnerships do not consider the social and environmental performance of the project, or of the partner, then they risk being accused of using public money to finance firms that are adding to the social or environmental problems they are meant to be addressing with those funds; not only may their reputation suffer, but legal issues could arise in future if officials disregard the corporate responsibility of recipients of government aid.

Motorola is one partner in Product (RED) raising finance for the Global Fund Against Aids, TB and Malaria]

Box 6 **Inspi(RED) fund-raising or (RED)wash? The case of Product(RED)™ (Exercise B)**

When Ivory Coast football captain Didier Drogba stepped onto the pitch at the 2010 World Cup, his boots sported red laces. It was the latest demonstration of his support for the partnership between sports brand Nike and Product(RED)™ to raise awareness and money for HIV/AIDS work in Africa. Nike sold red laces under the banner 'Lace Up. Save Lives', with all profits going to HIV/AIDS-related organisations.[a]

Launched in 2006 by U2 singer and activist Paul Hewson, popularly known as Bono, Product(RED)™ is 'a brand designed to engage business and consumer power in the fight against AIDS in Africa'. It works with 'world's best brands' to make unique (RED)-branded products and direct up to 50% of its gross profits to the Global Fund against AIDS, TB and Malaria, to fund African HIV/AIDS programmes focused on the health of women and children. (RED)™, however, 'is not a charity or campaign' but 'an economic initiative that aims to deliver a sustainable flow of private sector money to the Global Fund', according to its fact sheet. Product partners include Converse, Gap, Motorola, Emporio Armani, Apple, Hallmark, Dell, Microsoft and American Express, raising more than $150 million; (RED) reports that more than 5 million people have been reached with testing, counselling, treatment and other services through support from the Global Fund and (RED)™.[b]

The advertising of the brand has been substantial, even featuring during prime-time TV coverage of the 2008 SuperBowl in the United States. As the initiative has grown in size, some have challenged its appropriateness. The *New York Times* questioned the effectiveness of a system that involved companies spending more on advertising than they generated as donations to (RED)™.[c] In response, (RED)™ emphasised that it is a business, not a charity. A more important issue, therefore, is how much an intermediary company such as Persuaders LLC, the owner of Product(RED)™, should receive from the process. They do not divulge the fees they are paid to set up the product partnerships, or what levels of accountability they aspire to in operational →

a www.nike.com/nikefootball/red
b www.joinred.com/FAQ
c select.nytimes.com/mem/tnt.html?_r=3&pagewanted=1&tntget=2008/02/06/
   business/06red.html&tntemail0=y&emc=tnt&oref=login

issues such as their own overheads and salaries, which has led to criticisms over lack of transparency.[d]

Another concern has been raised by some NGOs about the influence of (RED)™, and its corporate partners, on the Global Fund. (That fund is governed by rules to ensure that human need, not donor interest, determines the activities it supports.) However, (RED)™ wanted to promote itself to consumers by highlighting who was benefiting. So a compromise was reached: (RED)™ could identify itself with projects in Africa, but not further. Meanwhile, careful procedures were put in place when a participating company connects to a specific project. In subsequent years further specificity has been allowed, including specific countries and types of intended beneficiary. Non-(RED)™ donors to the fund are not able to brand their philanthropy in the same way. A non-(RED)™ donor's request for co-branding could cause problems for the system of needs-driven grant making.

Another set of questions arose concerning the corporate responsibility of product partners. A UN study found that corporations may be undermining the global fight against AIDS due to the impacts of their value chains on the conditions for HIV transmission and progression. These corporate partners may not even be seeking to address these.[e] Take the case of Motorola, a (RED)™ partner. The production, shipment, retail and financing of the Motorola(RED)™ phones involves activities that both increase and decrease the likelihood of people and communities to be exposed to infection and to succumb to full-blown AIDS. Cobalt, mostly from Africa, particularly Congo, is required in all mobile phones. Mining of minerals such as cobalt has been key to the spread of AIDS in Africa. Therefore, the existence of mines and the mining companies' policies and programmes, not only for its operations but the workplace and community as well, are important in the fight against HIV.

In response to concerns about their product partners, (RED)™ adopted some principles, including that '(RED) respects its employees and asks its partners to do the same with their employees and the people who help make their products or deliver their services' and that '(RED) promotes HIV/AIDS workplace policies and practices'. However, in 2010 the Persuaders LLC is not listed as a member of the Global Business Coalition against HIV/AIDS and nor is Motorola, unlike its

→

d For instance, see Sarah Dadush, 'Profiting in (RED): Innovative Development Finance or a Symptom of Inadequate Regulation?' (IILJ, 2010; www.iilj.org/research/documents/FDC.Dadush.pdf) and Amy Elizabeth Martin, 'Seeing (RED): A Qualitative Analysis of the Product (RED) Campaign and Integration of Public Relations and Marketing Theory' (Louisiana State University, 2008): 64 (etd.lsu.edu/docs/available/etd-04162008-141353).

e Jem Bendell, *Waking Up to Risk? Corporate Responses to HIV/AIDS in the Workplace* (Geneva: UNRISD, 2003).

competitors Telkom, Siemens and Nokia.[f] The company's CSR reports have not mentioned working on HIV/AIDS workplace policies and programmes with their suppliers. Social auditor Verité has called for the company to do more on promoting awareness of Motorola's code on various aspects of labour relations, with its suppliers. This code did not provide evidence that Motorola has improved the impacts of its value chain to a degree that could give confidence in a statement that one of its products is 'Designed to Eliminate AIDS in Africa', as their advertising claims.

Many people are concerned about HIV/AIDS because they care about health and human rights. Therefore, the broader impact on or contribution of Motorola to health and human rights can be relevant. On the one hand, there is growing evidence of the benefits for poor communities of having access to mobile telephony, with benefits for incomes, and therefore nutrition and health. On the other hand, there are still concerns about the long-term health effects of mobile phones.

Others raised concerns that (RED)™ could be sending a message to the public that the current economic system and its large corporations are part of the solution, rather than an obstacle, to social challenges like HIV/AIDS. Denmark-based sociologists Lisa Ann Richey and Stefano Ponte argued that (RED)™ 'masked the social and environmental relations of trade and production that underpin poverty, inequality and disease'.[g] Political economic analysis of the reasons why governments, communities and individuals have been unable to protect and look after themselves adequately raises questions about the current system of corporate globalisation.[h] One campaign group argued that 'simply buying an item or advertising support for a cause will not solve an epidemic . . . It takes thinking more critically and consciously about how we consume.' They launched a counter-campaign that raised funds for HIV/AIDS in Africa through the reclaiming and recycling of consumer products, branded with a (RE)D – not (RED)™ – logo. They argued that (RED)™

> implies that corporations, branding and consumption are a necessary and healthy part of involvement in a cause . . . [Such] marketing is not only manipulative, but damaging. It claims to erase any guilt from shopping by offering products that aim to be not only ethically neutral but activist in nature . . . 'This is for the greater good' supplants doubts about the questionable origins or future life of an object.

→

f   www.gbcimpact.org/member-profiles

g   Lisa Ann Richey and Stefano Ponte, 'Better (Red)™ than Dead? Celebrities, Consumption and International Aid', *Third World Quarterly* 29.4 (2008): 711–29.

h   Bendell, *Waking Up to Risk?*

Some might regard Product(RED)™ to be a form of REDwash, a corporate pretence at social benefit, similar to 'greenwash', the pretence of environmental friendliness.

Bono and Bobby Shriver's wholly owned Persuaders LLC, which owns the trademark Product(RED)™, took steps against the (RE)D initiative. Persuaders asserted that their critics should be legally accountable for any breach of copyright, and the (RE)D initiative dropped its anti-RED brand. However, others may question to whom the Persuaders LLC, or its owners, should be accountable to with respect to their product partners' direct and indirect impact on public health.[i]

___

Reflect on, or discuss:

- What could be done to allay concerns about the transparency, governance and influence of this partnership?
- Could the product partners become a force for public health through the way they run their core business?
- Assuming good intentions, what strategic and management competences might the founders of Product(RED) have benefited from during its first years?

___

i   All quotes and information sourced from www.theglobalfund.org and www.joinred. com, accessed July 2008.

Perhaps your reflections or discussions during the exercise on Product(RED) revealed the following themes:

- As we look into the causes of a particular social or environmental problem, or consider the motivations for being concerned about such problems, the broader impact of a corporation's activities on society comes into focus

- As this occurs so judgements are made about the 'reality' of the political economy underlying a social problem, and about how relevant the more systemic analyses are to practical action

Some may consider that the more systemic analyses of problems are too 'ideological' and 'impractical', and in some cases less 'moral', because they do not lead to practical, immediate action to benefit needy individuals. However, others may regard critical analysis to be essential. Despite the difficulties of operationalising a more systemic analysis of the relationship of business to a particular social problem, the limited impact of what might at first appear to be 'practical' approaches may necessitate a broader agenda. This guidebook can help that development of perspective.

Faced with concerns about how their partnerships relate to some of the deeper causes of the problems they are working on, practitioners in public-interest organisations tend to respond in one of four ways:

- **Deny**. Ignore or argue against the relevance to their own partnership of a deeper analysis of systemic causes of the problems they address

- **Delineate**. Decide not to work on that analysis explicitly but ensure that one's partnering work does not undermine work on that deeper agenda. This can involve incorporating guidelines on how the partnership may or may not be promoted

- **Divide**. Encourage work on systemic causes but not with a corporate partner. For example, many NGOs work on trade and economic justice issues quite separately from their work with companies

- **Direct**. Explore with corporate partners how they might find a commercially viable way of working on the deeper agenda of systemic causes for the problems faced. This may not be possible, but some aspects of a more systemic agenda might have commercial benefits, if not others

The fourth approach underlies this guidebook. It has been embraced by enough practitioners over the past decade to reveal an evolution towards second-generation partnerships with businesses that seek to change internal operations to help address public problems. The main focus of change specified in internal and public communications about such partnerships is normally the internal operations of corporate partners and their suppliers. These forms of partnership generated the excitement of originality of cross-sector partnering in the mid 1990s. In many cases they represented a coming-together of previously conflicting parties, illustrating a paradigm shift in business strategy towards society and in the tactics of civil society. Examples profiled in the first book included: the Environment Defense Fund working with McDonald's on their food packaging; WWF-UK engaging a group of wood product manufacturers, traders and retailers to ensure their supplies came from well-managed forests; WWF-International collaborating with Unilever to create a certification system for sustainable fisheries.[12]

Since then, various types of second-generation partnership have emerged:

- **Exchange partnerships**, where organisations swap staff in order to help the organisations learn about each other and improve processes accordingly. One example is HSBC and WWF, whose staff have gone on to secondment, sometimes deciding to permanently remain

- **Product partnerships**, where organisations collaborate to bring new products to market that are socially or environmentally preferable to existing options. An early example was Greenpeace working with the German firm Foron in the early 1990s to produce Green Freeze fridges that did not use chlorofluorocarbons (CFCs), thereby reducing damage to the ozone layer

- **Process partnerships**, where organisations collaborate to improve particular organisational processes, such as purchasing and supply. Two examples of this type of partnership were mentioned earlier – the Forest Trade Network and the Ethical Trading Initiative

- **Standards partnerships**, where organisations collaborate to establish social or environmental standards for products or processes. These often give rise to new organisations that oversee the development of the standard and systems for its application. Examples include the Global Reporting Initiative, Forest Stewardship Council (FSC) and Marine Stewardship Council. Some consider these third-generation partnerships, as they create wider change in the industry, something we return to below.

Partnerships can involve a mix of these different types. A management process partnership can lead to a product development or standards development partnership, and involve a staff exchange to help implement this work. WWF-UK created a management process partnership with companies to source timber from well-managed forests, which led to the effort to create a standard, through the FSC, and also to product development, such as WWF helping create One Planet Living housing communities using

---

12 David F. Murphy and Jem Bendell, *In the Company of Partners: Business, Environmental Groups and Sustainable Development Post-Rio* (Bristol, UK: The Policy Press, 1997).

sustainable timber, and involved staff exchanges between WWF and its partner companies.

Examples from forests and seas

In the early 1990s companies involved in the timber trade were coming under increasing pressure through public concern over tropical deforestation. Protests at, and boycotts of, do-it-yourself stores such as B&Q in the UK, combined with a lack of trust in company claims for the environmental credentials of their products, were posing a major business problem. WWF approached the industry, inviting them to collaborate on finding a solution, so that the companies could source all their wood and wood products from well-managed forests. A group of companies committed to that goal emerged, hosted by WWF, and they began collaborating to establish a system for credible endorsement of forests and their products: the Forest Stewardship Council (FSC). The UK-based club of companies provided inspiration for similar WWF partnerships with the timber trade worldwide. In 2009 the resultant Global Forest and Trade Network (GFTN) accounted for 16% of every forest product bought or sold internationally every year, with combined annual sales of US$66 billion. The participant companies manage over 20 million hectares of certified forest.[13]

Meanwhile, those engaged in marine products have initiated a similar a partnership. Officially launched in 1999, the Marine Stewardship Council (MSC) operates a system for the certification of fisheries as sustainable and the labelling of fish products. A decade on, there are over 2,366 seafood products available with the MSC eco-label, sold in more than 40 countries, in a market now estimated to be worth US$1.5 billion annually. Forty-two fisheries have been independently certified as meeting the MSC's environmental standard for sustainable fishing. Over 6 million tonnes of seafood are either certified or under assessment – nearly 7% of the world's total wild harvest.[14]

---

13 GFTN, *GFTN Newsletter* (November 2009): 11; gftn.panda.org/?179321/GFTN-Quarterly-Newsletter-November-2009.

14 MSCAnnualReport2008/2009(www.msc.org/documents/msc-brochures/annual-report-archive/MSC-annual-report-2008-09.pdf/view?searchterm=annual%20report).

Both these initiatives involved a public-interest organisation seeking to leverage the buying power of large companies such as B&Q and Unilever, in order to influence the social or environmental performance of whole supply chains in an industry, rather than simply seeking financial contributions. Some benefits for different parts of society are shown in **Box 8**.

Most often, such partnerships arise from concerns over the way in which companies, rather than public-interest organisations, have an impact on a particular social or environmental issue. For instance, it was labour conditions in supply chains of high-street retailers, not development charities, that gave rise to the work programme of the Ethical Trading Initiative (ETI). This initiative was founded to improve labour rights in companies supplying British companies, but the initiative also commits all its partners, including the NGOs themselves, to apply a base code of labour standards (see **Box 19**). Another illustration of how these forms of partnership often involve the public-interest organisation committing to upgrade internal operations in line with the partnership goals is WWF's work with businesses involved in the timber trade. For their part, the WWF national organisations also seek to apply the same standards in their own sourcing of wood products.

On occasion, the partnership even addresses a particular capacity development need of an NGO or UN agency. The case of Bhavishya Alliance is instructive since it involves large corporations such as Unilever, and public-interest organisations such as Unicef and the Government of India. The partners collaborate to address child malnutrition. One of its programme aims is 'system strengthening' and one initiative included a partnership project between Unilever and the Department of Health to improve the health supply chain, thereby increasing the availability of medicines at primary health centres.[15]

Such partnerships sometimes grow out of first-generation partnerships, as the partners begin to understand the importance of core business operations for the issues addressed by the partnership. Sometimes the partners also become aware that others outside the partnership in media and civil society are making those connections for them and calling for action. However, more often these partnerships grow out of conflict, either between the partners, or other public-interest organisations. When a company seeks a partnership with a public-interest organisation connected to an issue, which the company and another public-interest organisation has been in conflict with, the organisations should progress carefully and consult

---

15   www.bhavishya.org.in

with the participants in that conflict. For instance, more moderate NGOs, or NGOs founded by business, such as Business for Social Responsibility (BSR) or WBCSD, are often contacted to initiate projects, partly in response to pressures emanating from wider civil society. The case of the timber trade provides a useful example of how such a partnership can emerge from conflict.

Box 7 **Example of a second-generation partnership: the Ethical Trading Initiative**

The Ethical Trading Initiative (www.ethicaltrade.org) is a ground-breaking alliance of companies, trade unions, charities and campaigning organisations that work together to improve working conditions in global supply chains, based out of the UK. The ETI grew out of growing concern in the mid 1990s among UK civil society about working conditions in the factories and plantations providing products sold by UK firms, and a lack of clarity about what such companies should be asking of their suppliers. Many retailers adopted voluntary codes of conduct on worker welfare issues, but found that they had neither the public credibility, nor the necessary experience and skills, to address these issues alone. Many realised they needed the support of relevant civil-society organisations, in particular, trade unions and NGOs with expertise in labour issues and international development. Therefore, a group of NGOs, trade unions and British companies came together and proposed a new initiative, which received backing from the UK Department for International Development.

The ETI was formally established in 1998 to bring the combined knowledge and influence of relevant NGOs and the international trade union movement to work alongside companies in identifying and promoting good practice in code implementation. The initiative involved many of the UK's leading retailers, including Tesco, Sainsbury's and Marks & Spencer, as well as the International Trade Union Confederation and the UK's Trades Union Congress, along with a variety of NGOs, including CAFOD, CARE International UK, Oxfam GB, the Fairtrade Foundation and Women Working Worldwide (WWW).

Their first task was to agree a 'Base Code and Principles of Implementation' to provide a basic philosophy from which ETI participants could identify and develop good practice, and a generic standard for company performance. The Base Code contains nine clauses which reflect the key international standards on labour practices. The Principles of Implementation set out general principles shaping the implementation of that code.

The ETI requires all corporate members to submit annual progress reports on their code implementation activities. The ETI secretariat assesses the work of its members, and disengages poor performers if they do not respond to requests for improved efforts.

In the past decade the ETI has disseminated a raft of best-practice tools and guidance on ethical trade, and galvanised industry-wide alliances that have →

brought about change for workers. In 2009, its member companies reported over 84,520 separate improvements to workers' conditions across a base of 40,000 suppliers, which the secretariat estimated collectively improved the lives of over 8.6 million workers.[a] In its ten-year review conference, many participants agreed the need to adopt a more systems-oriented approach, seeking to support workers and their associations in pushing for better conditions at work, and to ensure that their own buying practices did not undermine the potential for good industrial relations.

a Ethical Trading Initiative, 'Results in 2008' (2009; www.eti.org.uk accessed February 2010).

Box 8 **Some illustrative benefits and limits of second-generation partnerships**

Group	Benefits	Limits
Public-interest organisations Civil-society groups, intergovernmental organisations and government agencies with a public purpose	Leveraging corporate expertise and support	Reduced credibility if charging for services, limited scalability if not
	Organisational learning	Low member or media interest
Business All forms of private-sector companies including finance	Organisational learning	Staff time and budget costs
	Risk management	Increasing complexity of business processes
Politicians Within government or in opposition, not directly involved in the partnership	Informed consumer choice	Diversity of new standards
	Increasing public awareness	Unaccountability of standards
Intended beneficiaries People whom partners claim to be helping through their partnership	New avenues of influence	Variable accountabilities
	Increased public awareness	Variable standards and forms of redress
Wider society The general public, not directly involved in the partnership	Consumption opportunities	Patchwork responses
	Innovation on public issues	Uncritical policy paradigm

The experience of the WWF Forest and Trade Network (FTN) highlights some of the limitations also shown in **Box 8**.[16] The 2006 report of the FTN in the UK showed that only 11% of the wood imports of its member companies were certified under the FSC system; 72% of imports were either of unknown origin or known but of unconfirmed legality. Much of this wood comes from regions of the world with particularly important forests for biodiversity.[17] Subsequent annual reports to the date of publication of this guidebook have not reported such aggregate percentages.

Meanwhile, almost 86% of all forests endorsed by the FSC worldwide are in temperate and boreal regions, not the tropical zones where rainforest deforestation poses the most acute challenge to biodiversity, climate change, soil depletion and the human rights of forest dwellers.[18] It was tropical deforestation that inspired the NGO campaigns and corporate responses in the early 1990s that led to the creation of the FSC.[19] As a result of the slow progress in tropical forests, the FSC has launched an effort aimed at 'Strengthening FSC National Initiatives'.[20] Tropical deforestation remains a major problem today. Some estimate about 100,000 km^2 are deforested each year, and another 100,000 km^2 are degraded. Only in the Congo Basin and some isolated areas of the Amazon Basin does the forest remain largely intact. Any reductions in the rate of deforestation represent increases in reforestation rather than reduction in destruction of primary forests, with their more important biodiversity.[21]

16   For a more detailed discussion of limitations, see Jem Bendell, *Barricades and Boardrooms* (Geneva: UNRISD, 2004).

17   WWF-UK, *The WWF-UK Forest and Trade Network Annual Report 2006/7* (www.wwf.org.uk/ftn/report.asp).

18   Global FSC Certificates: Type and Distribution, September 2009: 9 (www.fsc.org/facts-figures.html).

19   Murphy and Bendell, *In the Company of Partners*.

20   www.fsc.org/ppp-ni.html

21   Lecture on Global Deforestation (University of Michigan, 2010; www.globalchange.umich.edu/globalchange2/current/lectures/deforest/deforest.html).

3 Transcending limitations with a third generation of partnerships

The disappointing figures on tropical deforestation rates point to a key limitation with voluntary, market-based actions for social change: they rely on societal drivers – such as consumer, staff and investor awareness – to change business practice. These drivers, however, are not uniform, and so bad practice can continue.

The limitations of engaging individual companies is highlighted by the experience of Sudan since the early 1990s. That decade witnessed a surge in international campaigning for corporations to improve their social and environmental impacts in conflict-affected countries. In Sudan, western oil companies such as Talisman were targeted by NGOs condemning the detrimental influence of oil development in the long-standing civil war. Most of the companies ceased operations due to pressure from Western consumers and investors. However, by 2005 it had become clear that Asian national oil companies were expanding their presence in Sudan. Being less in the spotlight and driven by rising demands for natural resources, such companies appeared to be less amenable to civil-society pressure. As a result the engagement with Western oil companies did little to affect the course of the conflict in Sudan. Rather, an international response was necessary. Unfortunately the oil companies, their adversaries and partners among civil society did not address the global oil governance challenge that resolving the Sudan conflict requires. A focus on the ethics of individual companies' internal operations did not in this case contribute to tackling the public issue.

Companies that do not voluntarily seek higher social and environmental performance can be tough competitors, and put price pressure on more responsible companies. In addition, business executives may only be able to go so far in taking on short-term costs to achieve long-term benefit, or in internalising negative externalities for the benefit of the economy as a whole. For instance, a factory might be able to offer decent working conditions, but not afford to pay a living wage, given existing client demands on price, quality and flexibility. One company that began to see the limitations of voluntary action was the US footwear and sports apparel company Nike. The company found that its competitors were not all investing as much in improving working conditions, and that consumers and media were still sceptical of their efforts. Facing these challenges, Nike could have scaled back its corporate responsibility efforts, but instead decided to raise them to a new and more systemic level. In 2005 Nike's mission became 'to effect positive, systemic change in working conditions within the footwear, apparel and equipment industries'. As management strategist Peter Senge explains, 'leadership exists when people are no longer victims of circumstances but participate in creating new circumstances'.[1] As a result, Nike is working with public-interest organisations on challenges such as supporting the capacity of labour inspectorates in source countries. For instance, Nike is collaborating with the International Labour Organisation's factory improvement programme in Vietnam.[2]

Third-generation partnerships focus not only on improvements within, and benefits to, the participants, but also on changing the barriers and drivers that constitute their operational contexts and those of similar organisations. That way, the impact of the partnership is both deep and broad enough to address the societal challenges involved. Such partnerships arise from a recognition of the limits of collaboration that relies on voluntary corporate action, and a greater focus on the role of external factors such as finance, government, consumers and media. Whereas second-generation

1   Peter Senge, 'Introduction', in Joseph Jaworski, *Synchronicity: The Inner Path of Leadership* (San Francisco: Berrett-Koehler, 1990): 3.

2   Ethisphere (2008) *How Nike is Changing The World, One Factory At a Time*, 26 March 2008; ethisphere.com/how-nike-is-changing-the-world-one-factory-at-a-time.

partnerships came about because of a frustration with traditional public policy process by partners – where NGOs often wanted more action, while companies often wanted less – the third generation involves bringing public governance issues back into focus.

Although progress has been limited in some areas, such as the global governance of the oil industry, progress has been made in other areas, such as forest conservation and anti-corruption. There are signs of an evolving approach in the UK Forest and Trade Network (FTN). The secretariat notes that members can 'bring about consumer awareness of the problems of illegal logging, and how responsibly managed forest products can help tackle this issue'. Promoting change is 'through the ability to lobby key stakeholders to bring about changes to tackle deforestation and illegal logging'.[3] Discussions are ongoing about whether to specify targets on these issues, and methods for grading companies on their performance. One remarkable development in this broader focus was the lobbying of the European Commission by UK FTN member companies to achieve a ban in 2010 on illegally felled timber into the EU, with certificates such as the FSC being one means for demonstrating legal compliance. One focus for advocacy and lobbying are intergovernmental responses to climate change. The UK FTN has not been vocal on this, but working through the GFTN WWF and its partner companies have been calling for intergovernmental agreement to combat climate change and provide additional funds to stem deforestation.[4]

Some of the world's largest companies in the World Economic Forum are taking 'collective efforts to address systemic challenges, such as improving the quality of public education, reforming healthcare delivery, strengthening the financial sector, and building mechanisms to tackle corruption'. Respondents to the Forum's survey identified 'building the framework conditions for good governance' as the most important area for partnerships. These include efforts to 'spread industry-wide or global standards for accountability, transparency, and responsible business practices' and 'to help strengthen public institutions and administrative capacity'.[5] At the UN Global Compact (UNGC), interest of participants in systemic change is reflected by the 2010 launch of the *Blueprint for Sustainability Leadership*,

---

3 WWF-UK, *The WWF-UK Forest and Trade Network Annual Report 2006/7* (www.wwf.org.uk/ftn/report.asp).

4 See press releases from GFTN, including 'WWF Recommendations for climate finance for the G20 Summit' (wwf.panda.org/about_our_earth/all_publications/?193921/WWF-Recommendations-for-the-G20).

5 WEF, *Partnering for Success: Business Perspectives on Multistakeholder Partnerships* (Geneva: WEF, 2005): 6.

which identifies ways that companies affect enabling conditions of fair and sustainable markets.[6]

Therefore we are witnessing the emergence of a range of third-generation partnerships, involving advocacy, lobbying, enterprise, education, finance and, potentially, standardisation (**Box 9**).

Box 9 **Types of third-generation partnership**

Third-generation partnerships seek to transform the factors constituting the contexts of the partners, and similar organisations, to enable them to move further towards their social and environmental goals. They include:

- **Advocacy partnerships**, where organisations collaborate to change personal attitudes and behaviours on social or environmental issues and thus drive change in the business

- **Lobbying partnerships**, where organisations collaborate to influence politician or civil servant understandings of social and environmental issues and encourage agreement at national or intergovernmental levels for new regulations or funds

- **Enterprise partnerships**, where organisations collaborate to establish or improve enterprises that meet unmet social needs, or general needs in sustainable ways, and thus generate surpluses to reinvest to achieve scale and thereby disrupt problematic economic activities or incumbent companies

- **Education partnerships**, where organisations collaborate to change the curricula of organisations that offer teaching and training on management, to ensure social and environmental factors are incorporated, and therefore better inform the practices of executives

- **Finance partnerships**, where organisations collaborate to influence the operations of financial institutions on environmental, social and governance issues, with the intention of influencing the practices of invested corporations as well as financing businesses necessary for social or environmental change

- **Standards partnerships**, where organisations collaborate to establish social or environmental standards for products or processes. These often give rise to new organisations that oversee the development of the standard and systems for its application. These partnerships can also be considered second-generation partnerships, as they do not always focus on how to create change in the whole industry, and their efficacy in creating such change depends on strategic decisions within the resultant standards bodies

6 www.unglobalcompact.org/docs/news_events/8.1/Blueprint.pdf

Box 10 **The Allianz Partnership**

Key to third-generation partnerships is that the corporate partner seeks to play a role in wider social change in ways that also make commercial sense. One way to do that is to support enterprises that seek to address social needs in new ways, and in doing so improve one's own staff competencies.

Allianz is a leader in insurance and financial services with nearly 155,000 employees worldwide. It identified an opportunity to utilise its own internal quality management methodology, known as OPEX – operational excellence – to give back to the community while supporting the growth of its own employees. Together with the social enterprise adviser Volans, they created a global leadership development programme, Social OPEX, that prepares leaders and managers for the future and also to have a stronger and lasting impact on society. This programme brings trained experts from Allianz together with established social enterprises to tackle their current business challenges, improve business operations and increase their overall social impact. At the same time, it benefits Allianz employees by building their innovation quotient, encouraging entrepreneurial thinking, applying their skills in a different environment and acquiring leadership skills.

MyBnk, one of the organisations involved, is a social enterprise that aims to increase financial literacy and develop young people's enterprise skills by giving them hands-on experience in organising, running and using a bank. Allianz and MyBnk worked together to design a franchising framework that will allow the MyBnk proposition to be deployed both in provincial UK and internationally. Together, the team created a robust and documented franchising process along with a blueprint for a partnership model.

Lily Lapenna, CEO of MyBnk, explained how:

> the OPEX framework allowed us both to see things anew and to see a logic to a process that was both daunting and confusing previously. The OPEX exercises have proved to be extremely effective, straightforward and user friendly. I feel I could replicate some of them and apply them to other areas of my work.

Paul Achleitner, Chief Financial Officer of Allianz SE and sponsor of the Social OPEX programme, believes 'those companies who are more attuned to current and upcoming social and environmental issues have a competitive advantage over those who narrowly focus on a single bottom line'. John Elkington of Volans concurs that:

> companies that will lead in this changing economy will be those that understand social dimensions of doing business, ones that can

gather insight from working with leading innovators, and learn to deliver products and services with limited resources. Responding quickly to these challenges will require responsible leadership.[a]

Allianz is also working with the NGO, CARE International. After using the tools in this guidebook, the private-sector team has increased its efforts to engage companies in more transformative ways. Developing finance partnerships can be one way of creating wider impact. Care and Bajaj Allianz – the Indian arm of Allianz – are now working together to provide insurance for people in southern India who were affected by the tsunami. 'Together, we help communities understand how insurance can help families and communities cope with the risks they face – from illness to major disasters – so that they can cope after a disaster,' explains Care's Tim Bishop. The health insurance scheme offers packages which protect people against natural disasters or accidents for an equivalent of under 10 US cents a day – an affordable rate even for those who earn less than $2 day. For people without savings, social security or access to financial services, the securing of insurance can enable them to access a wider range of financial services, develop some savings, avoid loan sharks and develop their micro enterprises. Therefore Tim Bishop believes that the work with Allianz 'has started to present some of the most compelling recent data in terms of "system-change" collaboration'.[b]

---

a   All data and quotes provided by personal communication with John Elkington, July 2010.

b   Personal communication with Tim Bishop, July 2010.

Some leading examples of lobbying-focused third-generation partnerships focus on climate change. In 2007 in the United States one such partnership was launched with ten major companies, including General Electric, DuPont, Alcoa, Caterpillar and BP, with leading NGOs such as Environmental Defense and the Natural Resources Defense Council. The United States Climate Action Partnership (USCAP) is:

> a group of businesses and leading environmental organizations that have come together to call on the federal government to quickly enact strong national legislation to require significant reductions of greenhouse gas emissions. USCAP has issued a landmark set of principles and recommendations to underscore the urgent need for a policy framework on climate change.[7]

---

7   www.us-cap.org

The existence of such partnerships gives rise to some questions about accountability public policy making, which we explore later (see Chapter 6 and **Box 24**).

Advocacy partnerships can aim to influence attitudes among the general public. For instance, the UN High Commission for Refugees has convened a Council of Business Leaders to help it innovatively pursue its mandate, which includes advocating for the refugee cause. Companies involved include Nike, Microsoft, PricewaterhouseCoopers, Merck and Manpower. One initiative from this council is ninemillion.org, a worldwide, multi-year campaign aimed at raising awareness and funds for education and sport programmes for refugee children. While approximately $10 million of in-kind donations have been invested, a key outcome of the campaign is the raising of the profile of the agency and the cause of refugees, particularly among the youth.

Advocacy partnerships sometimes focus on changing attitudes and behaviours among business executives. One example is the UNGC and World Bank initiative on 'Collective Action', a process of cooperation between various stakeholders with the aim to jointly counter corruption.

> Through such alliance of like-minded organizations the problem can be approached and resolved from multiple angles and the impact of individual action can be increased. Collective Action means that companies, governments and civil society organizations join

TRANSCENDING LIMITATIONS WITH A THIRD GENERATION OF PARTNERSHIPS forces in order to guarantee transparency in business, e.g. in public procurement processes.[8]

Enterprise partnerships, where organisations collaborate to establish new enterprises to meet unmet social needs or general needs in sustainable ways, can thus generate surpluses to reinvest to achieve scale and thereby disrupt problematic economic activities or incumbent companies. One of the best and most famous examples of a public-interest organisation adopting enterprise solutions to transform social problems is the Grameen group of businesses from Bangladesh whose founder, Muhammad Yunus, received the Nobel Peace Prize in 2006.[9] In addition to its well-known work on microfinance, providing small loans to groups of women to start businesses, Grameen is engaged in sustainable energy, agriculture and telecommunications, partnering with a range of international companies to develop new enterprise solutions. For example, providing telecommunications was recognised as an important means for enhancing the economic and social development of rural areas in Bangladesh, where isolation and poor infrastructure are the norm.[10] With this in mind, the Grameen Bank established GrameenPhone as a joint venture with Norway's Telenor.[11] GrameenPhone makes telephone services available to rural villages in Bangladesh, with one member of a community taking a loan to acquire the handset, which is financed by charging the rest of the community for access. After almost ten years of operation, there are now 50 million telephone users in the country, 80% of these mobile phones, making GrameenPhone the leading telecommunications provider in Bangladesh.[12] Other similar innovations include Grameen Foundation's partnership with the firm Qualcomm to create a Village Phone Microfranchising Program, PT RUMA, where a cellular airtime sales kit enables an entrepreneur to sell prepaid airtime from 11 telecommunications companies to their community. This initiative is transformative as it helps people who previously could not afford it to access

---

8   Collective Action, 'Collective Action in the Fight Against Corruption' (2010; www. fightingcorruption.org).

9   Nobel Foundation, 'The Nobel Peace Prize 2006', available from nobelprize.org/ nobel_prizes/peace/laureates/2006. See also Jem Bendell and Wayne Visser, 'World Review', *Journal of Corporate Citizenship* 13 (2005) for other discussions on the Grameen group of businesses.

10   GrameenPhone 'Every Opportunity Counts: Community Information Centre', available from www.grameenphone.com/index.php?id=426.

11   *Ibid.*

12   *Ibid.*

key information related to market prices, among other issues.[13] The UN's World Food Programme is working with Unilever and Kraft Foods on a five-year, US$50 million public–private partnership that seeks to eradicate child malnutrition. Somewhat oddly called 'Project Laser Beam' (PLB), it is initially targeting Bangladesh and Indonesia, which have high rates of child malnutrition. The project centres around three main pillars: food, hygiene and behavioural change. It is a complex partnership, including fortification of food with micro-nutrients, products to nutritionally supplement a child's diet, ready-to-use foods requiring no water or cooking, sanitation and hand-washing, access to clean water, de-worming, immunisation, therapeutic feeding for the severely malnourished, education on the benefits of breast-feeding, and nutrition education. The philosophy behind the partnership is to create financially self-sustaining solutions to child malnutrition and thus achieve a lasting scale. These forms of partnership are important for social development, and we explore the implications in greater depth in Chapter 7.

One academic initiative seeking to catalyse these third-generational partnerships is ELIAS – Emerging Leaders Innovate Across Sectors – a global innovation and learning community that develops regional platforms for facilitating multi-stakeholder innovation across entire systems, to address specific thematic or geographic concerns. The methodology includes a year-long leadership course where people are helped to become leaders in systemic change and then supported by the alumni network to implement systems-change oriented collaborations. One example of the outcomes of this programme comes from the Philippines, where an ELIAS fellow from Unilever teamed up with former colleagues working in the NGO sector to form MicroVentures, a support organisation that advises and finances women micro-entrepreneurs in the Philippines by leveraging the Unilever business and its network at the community level.[14]

The finance sector is another area where third-generation societal partnerships are emerging. This is because participants in a range of existing partnerships have realised that if they want to change the way business does business they have to change the way money makes money. According to Björn Stigson, president of the World Business Council for Sustainable Development: 'Financial markets are key to the pursuit of sustainable development . . . if financial institutions do not understand and reward sustain-

---

13   Business Civic Leadership Center (BCLC), 'Partnership Award Finalist – Qualcomm and Grameen Foundation'; www.usibc.com/bclc/awards/2010_partnership_qualcomm.htm.

14   The Presencing Institute, 'ELIAS Update' (2009); www.presencing.com/capacity-building/elias.shtml#.

able behaviour, progress in developing more sustainable business practices will be slow.' As awareness of this grows, we may be on the cusp of a 'capital turn' in civil society that will have as significant an effect on business as the 'corporate turn' of civil society in the early 1990s, when NGOs began engaging business more energetically.[15]

A key constituency and potential ally for public-interest organisation goals are institutional investors, who are meant to take a long-term view of asset appreciation. Within this sector the pension funds are key. This is because people pay into a pension fund in order to secure a quality of life when they retire, yet these deposits are often doing the exact opposite, funding companies to exhaust the natural capital needed in years to come. People save for the long term, but that money is most often managed for the short term by financial firms focused on generating billions of dollars in bonuses. Consequently, most people's pensions are putting the planet into retirement. Yet they could give it new life, if engaged to drive more sustainable business practices and regulations. Fortunately a range of initiatives has emerged in recent years to tackle the problem of short-termism in capital markets and the ignoring of social and environmental concerns.

- The Equator Principles now involve most large international banks

- The Marathon Club is a group of investors looking at ways to encourage investment for the long term

- The Enhanced Analytics Initiative (EAI) commits its members, which include BNP Paribas, USS, Investec and Hermes, to spend 5% of their brokerage fees with firms that focus on extra-financial indicators

- The UN Principles for Responsible Investment (UNPRI) has signatories who now account for about US$20 trillion assets under management

Until now most of these initiatives have not involved public-interest organisations. The UNPRI brings together financial institutions, and apart from the UN which hosts the initiative, public-interest organisations are not involved unless they sign up as asset owners. One initiative is seeking a cross-sectoral third-generation approach. Seeing the need for more transformative cross-sectoral dialogues on the financial system, in 2007 I worked WWF-UK's Jen Morgan on the idea for what became the Finance Innovation Lab. Run as a partnership between WWF-UK and the Institute of Chartered

---

15 Jem Bendell, *Barricades and Boardrooms* (Geneva: UNRISD, 2004): 19.

Accountants in England and Wales, the Lab brings together stakeholders and experts in the global financial system to explore what form of financial system would enable a fair and sustainable world economy. It considers how to mainstream the integration of social and environmental value in all financial services and products, including whether a fundamental reordering of the rights and duties of capital and processes of money creation may be required, and the necessary roles for all stakeholders in reshaping the system accordingly.[16]

16   www.thefinancelab.org

4 Assessing your partnering

For partnerships to evolve requires that the partners themselves progress in their own understanding of effective collaboration. For business, this means a widening of the issues and individuals that business people accept as part of their responsibility. For public-interest organisations it involves a development in the way they target the market, and may even require an evolution in the way they understand their own organisational effectiveness and responsibility. Understanding, identifying and influencing these stages of development are important for planning how to create more systemic societal partnerships. This is the focus of the following sections and exercises. To begin with you can assess your current stage of partnering, with **Exercise C (Box 11)**.

Box 11 **Assessing your generation of partnerships (Exercise C)**

This exercise enables you to reflect on the forms of partnership that you are, or have been, engaged in. To begin, select a partnership that you were or are engaged with. Then complete this table and add up your scores. With a colleague, discuss what generation your partnership might be and your response to that.

No.	Is your engagement with companies:	Defi-nitely: 2 points	Some-what or some-times: 1 point	No/ don't know: 0 points	Score
1	Called a partnership by your organisation				
2	Called a partnership by the corporation(s)				
3	Generating revenues for your organisation				
4	Being communicated by the partners to other stakeholders				
5	Promoting operational changes by the company concerning their impact on the issues				
6	Promoting organisational change within your public-interest organisation (rather than programmatic change)				
7	Working towards an agreed time frame for operational improvements by the company				
8	Involving public reporting of progress towards partnership goals				
9	Involving independent evaluation of performance				
10	Providing opportunities for staff exchanges				

11	Educating stakeholders about the need for greater progress on the issue addressed by the partnership				
12	Influencing mainstream industry standards				
13	Influencing national public policy				
14	Influencing intergovernmental processes				
	TOTALS				

Add up your final total and compare it to this key:

0 to 2 points	**not a 'partnership'**
3 to 8 points	**a first-generation partnership**
9 to 21 points	**a second-generation partnerships**
22 to 28 points	**a third-generation partnership**

In their 2005 report on partnerships, the World Economic Forum notes that companies are at various stages of readiness for partnering: companies that are yet to be convinced of the business case; companies that are looking to get more actively engaged; and companies that are leading the field towards more systemic approaches.[1] The differences of approach to partnering reflect differing corporate approaches to their social responsibilities, of which there are various models advanced in academia and by consultants. One of the most relevant models for our purposes here was developed by Simon Zadek, who wrote about the three generations of corporate citizenship. He described how companies were moving focusing on giving to good causes, to improving their own operations in line with that cause, to eventually seeking to be a partner in affecting significant positive change in

---

1   WEF, *Partnering for Success: Business Perspectives on Multistakeholder Partnerships* (Geneva: WEF, 2005): 41–2.

society.[2] The UK consultancy SustainAbility found a similar progression in the corporate strategy of leading corporate responsibility reporters.[3]

The key aspects of this progression are synthesised in **Diagram III**. At the base is the strategy of ignoring one's social responsibilities. Many companies worldwide, both large and small, appear to ignore their social and environmental performance beyond mere legal compliance, which is itself a struggle to some. The next stage is philanthropy, where companies give funds to good causes as a way of giving something back to the community. The luxury industry in particular has understood its social responsibilities in this way, using celebrities for glamorous charity events, and not always looking closely at how their own operations affect the issues that their philanthropy is seeking to address. This approach also predominates in much of Asia, where corporate social responsibility is often defined entirely by charitable donations.

The next stage is reputation management, the beginnings of contemporary corporate responsibility. The potential risk to brand arising from negative news on social or environmental problems has been a key driver of change since Shell faced a consumer backlash over the proposed sinking of the Brent Spar oil platform in the North Atlantic and their operations in Nigeria during the mid 1990s. At this level of strategy, businesses can begin exploring possible second-generation societal partnerships. Many commentators argue that oil companies like BP and Shell remain within this stage of social responsibility, despite their claims to a more strategic approach to innovating new energy solutions, and to applying pressure for action on climate change. This is an example where rhetoric and reality can be debated, and where expressing a high level of social responsibility may be a public relations strategy rather than reflecting a genuine agenda. It also highlights how different parts of the same corporate group can have different approaches to social responsibility, and how implementation remains a major challenge for senior management in global companies.

---

2   Zadek also suggested in presentations at the Cambridge Programme for Industry that this implied three generations of partnership. In his framework the first level is a project partnership that seeks to deliver a practical benefit to a specific target group or environmental concern; the second level is a partnership that shares more resources and where a learning agenda is central to the partnership, leading to wider benefits and outcomes for the partners and their sectors; the third level is a partnership that strives to change the rules. This is a similar framework to the one advanced here, although I concentrate on whether the partnership focuses on the internal operations or external contexts, or both, of the organisations that partner.

3   SustainAbility, *Gearing Up: From Corporate Responsibility to Good Governance and Scalable Solutions* (London: SustainAbility, 2004).

Strategic responsibility is the next stage up the pyramid. This is where a company recognises that higher social and environmental performance can help organisational performance. It improves staff recruitment, retention and motivation, as well as relations with suppliers, communities, investors and other stakeholder groups. One company that appears to be working with this approach is L'Oréal, the world's largest cosmetics and beauty company, which has adopted a range of social and environmental performance targets. It also views these targets as a way of motivating staff, reducing costs and reassuring consumers.

The higher stage involves looking at social and environmental challenges as stimuli for innovating the business models and processes to succeed in future markets. This comes from a recognition that, while many of these challenges will grow in intensity and complexity, the power of human ingenuity to find ways of addressing them profitably will match these challenges. Osklen, the Brazilian fashion company, appears to be embracing this approach. Osklen's winter 2007 collection, 'amazon guardians', made use of organic wool, natural latex and fish leather. These fabrics were developed in partnership with Instituto-e, a not-for-profit organisation promoting sustainable human development in Brazil. WWF-Brazil has supported Instituto-e in promoting access to sustainable fabrics. Through Instituto-e's partnership with Osklen, the non-profit is entitled to a royalty from sales of products using these fabrics.[4] Two of the most famous companies expressing this approach to social responsibility are Nestlé and Unilever. Through innovative new products and business models, they focus on creating 'shared value' for both the company and poorer people. The growing attention to social enterprise, aspired to by Skoll Foundation, Acumen Fund, Schwab Foundation and others, is based on the belief that business innovation can address societal challenges. Its implications for corporate strategy are being more widely discussed: for instance, in John Elkington's best-selling book *The Power of Unreasonable People*.[5]

At the top of the pyramid of responsible business is 'societal leadership'. This approach arises from an understanding that all other stages do not necessarily lead a business to contribute to addressing the scale of a particular social or environmental challenge. The example of Nike's evolved

4   www.osklen.com.br

5   John Elkington and Pamela Hartigan, *The Power of Unreasonable People: How Social Entrepreneurs Create Markets That Change the World* (Boston, MA: Harvard Business Press, 2008).

approach to its corporate responsibility has been described above. The WEF explains that:

> even the most efficient, innovative and responsible companies can accomplish little in the absence of good governance. Rule of law, respect for human rights, freedom of speech and association, appropriate macroeconomic and microeconomic incentives, effective institutions, and more efficient administration and delivery of public goods are all essential for achieving both international goals and the creation of an enabling environment for private investment and enterprise.[6]

The CEO of Philips Van-Heusen explains that 'as business people we must continue the evolution of capitalism' and seek to shape societies in ways that benefit communities.[7]

When companies are at this stage they can engage in third-generation partnerships. Therefore, it is important to assess what stage a company is at, before seeking to explore and develop higher generations of partnership. **Exercise D** in **Box 12** can help you with that assessment.

---

6 WEF, *Partnering for Success*: 10.
7 *Ibid.*: 12.

Diagram III **Stages of responsible enterprise**

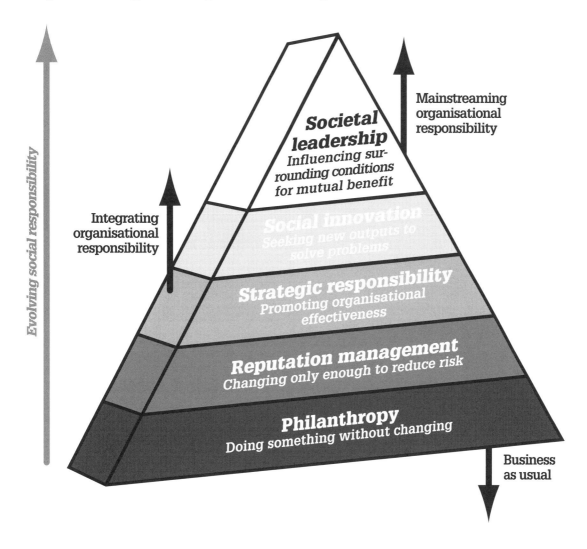

Evolving social responsibility

Mainstreaming organisational responsibility

Societal leadership
Influencing surrounding conditions for mutual benefit

Integrating organisational responsibility

Social innovation
Seeking new outputs to solve problems

Strategic responsibility
Promoting organisational effectiveness

Reputation management
Changing only enough to reduce risk

Philanthropy
Doing something without changing

Business as usual

Box 12 **Reflecting on a company's readiness to partner (Exercise D)**

This exercise is intended to help you reflect on what stage of corporate responsibility strategy a particular company is at, and therefore what partnership potential there may be. If possible, discuss the following questions with colleagues or even your counterpart in the company concerned:

1 What do I think is motivating the person(s) in the company I engage with? Why do they want to partner with my public-interest organisation?

2 What do I think is this person's own understanding of the causes of the problems we work on?

3 When talking of their interests and drivers, what do they most often identify? (e.g. risk, commitment, innovation, leadership, other interests/drivers)

4 What do I know about the business fundamentals of the company I engage with? For example, what are their core competencies and market strategies?

5 Is there significant reputational risk for the company arising from the issue that we work on together? Have they expressed this to me?

6 Are there significant opportunities for innovation arising from the issue that we work on? Have they expressed this to me?

7 Is the culture of the organisation suited to playing a societal leadership role? Are they connected enough?

The ability to engage in higher generations of partnership also depends on the approach of the public-interest organisation to markets and business. Some public-interest organisations, such as the Qatar educational charity Reach Out to Asia, appear to ignore the market and business. Others, such as the development charity Comic Relief, simply seek funds from corporate donors. Some, such as the environmental group People and Planet, see problems arising from the market and campaign against business. Others seek to compete in the marketplace with alternative enterprises, or promote alternative enterprise. An increasing number, such as WWF, engage companies on internal change, through the initiatives I have described earlier. Others engage them to drive market changes, either through consumer, staff and investor awareness, or through regulation and public policy. **Diagram IV** shows public-interest organisation approaches grouped into the following six categories:

- **Ignore** business and markets. The organisation does not concern itself with the market or business beyond passive receipt of donations

- **Critique**. The organisation researches and writes about impacts of companies and the market

- **Mobilise**. The organisation works with affected persons, their representatives, consumers, investors and so on to pressure companies and governments to act

- **Engage**. The organisation explores working with companies to improve their practices

- **Build and compete**. The organisation works to increase the capacity of producers and consumers to interact with markets in more beneficial ways, including local capacity development or creation of certification labels, and ultimately for social enterprise to compete with business as usual

- **Transform**. The organisation explores all forms of collaboration and contestation that can transform the fundamentals of markets, such as forms of financing, incorporation, regulation and trade law

Public-interest organisations sometimes use a multitude of these approaches for different business sectors and sometimes even the same sectors. For instance, the international environmental group Greenpeace ignores, competes, and engages business, depending on the issues and sectors involved. Unless the public-interest organisation is created specifically to work on responsible enterprise issues, the latter three approaches usually follow the first three. This progression is likely the result of learning about the limits and benefits of partnering, as outlined in this guidebook. Opinions differ as to whether a multitude of different approaches is important, with some arguing, as I did ten years ago, that unless some public-interest organisations are critiquing and mobilising against companies then there must be less of a business case for corporate action.[8]

---

8   A key concept here on the need for different tactics from civil society is 'civil regulation' which I developed in David F. Murphy and Jem Bendell, *Partners In Time?* (Geneva: UNRISD, 1999).

Take a moment to reflect on, or discuss, your own organisation's approach to targeting the market, using **Exercise E** in **Box 13**.

Then use **Exercise F** in **Box 14** to explore where there is interest within your existing partnerships for moving to a more transformative agenda. It provides a visual sense of where there is a pull or drag towards different generations of partnership, and can help you to decide where organisational development or communication efforts should occur in future.

Diagram IV **Stages of how public-interest organisations target the market**

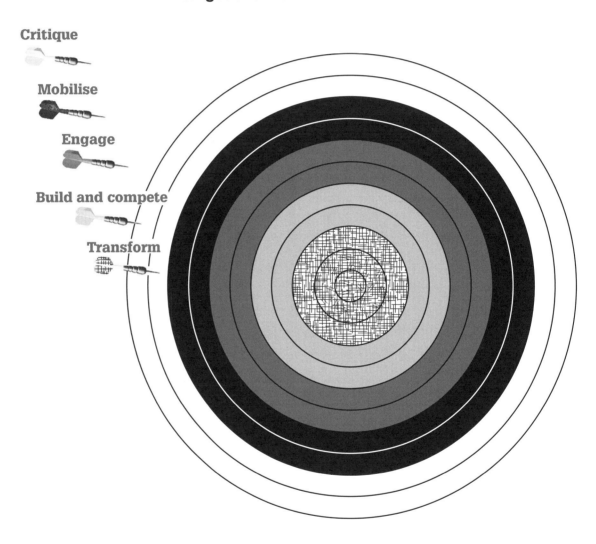

Critique

Mobilise

Engage

Build and compete

Transform

Box 13 **Assessing your organisational stage of targeting the market (Exercise E)**

This exercise is designed to allow you to assess your organisation's dominant approach to the market and business and thus ascertain what internal changes might be needed if you wish to evolve your partnering.

Answering the following questions may require you to access some internal reports, and to work with a blank sheet of paper. The questions can also be used as part of a discussion, once the necessary data is gathered.

1 Have any organisation-wide assessments of our engagement with business, industry and finance (perhaps also involving issues such as trade policy and regulation) been conducted?

- If yes, after reading this assessment, what stage of interacting with business and the market do you think describes the dominant approach of your organisation?

- If no, this suggests that the issue of corporate engagement is not a strategic priority, no matter what pronouncements have been made by senior management or directorate on this issue. This does not mean that there are not pockets within the organisation that may be pioneering different approaches . . .

- Are there projects that relate to either the 'build and compete' or 'transformation' approaches to the market and business?

- If yes, why are these not mainstream within the organisation, and does this matter?

2 Roughly what percent of annual expenditure is on work targeting the market? Note that this targeting can be through corporate engagement, or projects that critique business and mobilise its stakeholders, or that lobby for government or intergovernmental action on market issues, among others.

- Answering this question requires some access to organisation-wide budgets, and probably guesswork due to a lack of disaggregation of some categories of expenditure. This overall budget assessment is also important for then dividing unrestricted corporate donations on the basis of whether they fund market-related work or not, as part of the next question

- Roughly what percent of funds raised from corporate partners goes into work targeting the market, as defined and assessed above? →

- Typically these percent figures are very low. Comparing these figures with the percent of funds spent on advocacy and lobbying is, therefore, a useful yardstick to assess the extent to which your organisation is engaging market issues

3 In addition to assessments based on either quantity of practice (1 above), or quantity of expenditure (2 above), what other ways of assessing your organisation's overall approach to the market might there be?

- Try one of these. (Other ways might include assessments of organisational communications, such as annual reports, press releases, online information and statements from directors)

4 Do these different approaches give you a different or similar sense of your organisation's approach?

- If yes, which is more accurate for understanding your partnership readiness and why?
- If no, which factors are most crucial to determining your organisation's overall approach to partnering?
- What are the implications for internal organisational development of this assessment?

Box 14 **Mapping readiness to partner (Exercise F)**

This exercise gives you a visual sense of where there is a pull or drag towards different generations of partnership. This visual representation will help you to decide where organisational development or communication efforts should occur in future.

This exercise requires prior assessment of both the partnership readiness of corporations and your own organisation (from the previous exercises).

Choose one partnership your organisation is involved in that you know about. On the diagram below, for your chosen partnership, plot on each axis the following:

1 What do you think is the official position of one of the main corporate partners on the issue of their corporate responsibility?

2 What do you think is the position of your main liaison for the partnership in that company on the issue of their corporate responsibility

→

3 What do you think is the dominant position of your own organisation on approaches to business and markets?

4 What is your own position with regard to business and markets?

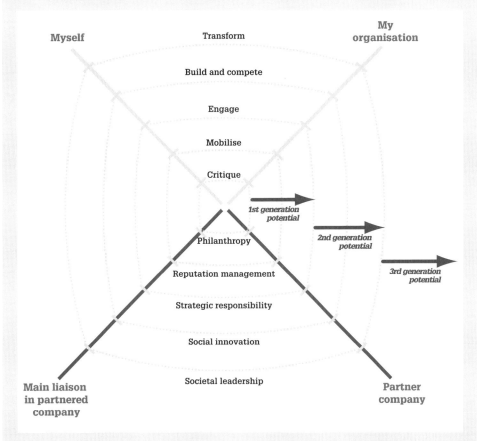

Then connect the points you have made on the diagram.

Further plots can be made on the same diagram, for different corporations involved in the same partnership, or different liaisons with the same company. After this, consider the following (perhaps making notes on separate pieces of paper):

- Where is there the least interest to expand the focus of the partnership (to evolve its 'generation')?
- What could be done to encourage them to change?
  - Are we doing this?
  - Who is responsible?
- How could I go about assessing whether alternative persons or organisations are more ready to expand the focus of a similar partnership?
- On the basis of my current knowledge, which alternative persons or organisations are likely to be more ready to expand the focus of a similar partnership?
- If other persons or organisations are more able to expand the focus of a partnership than myself or my organisation, what can I do to help?

The fitness framework for assessing partnerships

In the decade since I wrote a book about societal partnerships, these have progressed from novel experiments to mainstream approaches to public and commercial challenges. Consequently, partnerships necessarily require more evaluation of their performance and growing role in society. Evaluation can be conducted to improve decision-making, organisational learning, public relations, or to report to donors; it can also be used to inform strategic planning. Evaluation normally involves assessing whether an activity has been effective, efficient and appropriate against a stated objective or value. Sometimes, this leads to a re-evaluation of those objectives or values:

- Effectiveness of an activity is indicated by the extent that the outcomes achieve the set objectives. It asks the question: 'Are we having the impact we wanted'?

- Efficiency of an activity is indicated by the amount of outputs for the given inputs. This is important for the accountability of the resources being used. It asks the question: 'Are we having a sufficient impact for the costs involved?' An assessment of these costs can also include potential negative side effects and opportunity costs, as well as the financial inputs

- Appropriateness of an activity is indicated by the relevance of the objectives to the needs of participants and intended beneficiaries, and a wider assessment of the rightness of the means being used to deliver on those needs. It asks the question: 'Given the overall experience with the activity, should we continue doing this?'

A number of frameworks for evaluating partnerships have been developed in recent years. Some focus on the benefits derived by partners,[9] the rela-

---

9   Michael Warner, *Monitoring Tri-sector Partnerships* (Working Paper No. 13; London: Business Partners for Development Natural Resources Cluster, 2002; www.bpd-naturalresources.org).

tionships between partners,[10] the accountability of partnerships,[11] generating information to communicate to internal and external constituencies,[12] while others focus on the outcomes of partnerships.[13] Integrating these approaches, The Partnering Initiative proposes an evaluation framework covering the following dimensions of a partnership:

- **Impacts**. The achievement of shared and individual partner goals, and realising sustainable outcomes (this relates to partnership *effectiveness*)

- **Operations**. Partnership management, organisation and communications (this relates to partnership *efficiency*)

- **Partner benefit**. The partnership's added value to the partners and posing questions about alternatives to collaboration and unanticipated risks and costs of partnering (this relates to partnership *appropriateness*)[14]

This integrated approach responds to the need to become more systematic, strategic and comprehensive in evaluation so that partners can learn from their partnering experience. Key to such an approach will be to place as much attention on partnership appropriateness as matters of effectiveness and efficiency. Assessing an activity's appropriateness involves considering what has been learned about the challenges faced during the activity,

---

10   See Jennifer M. Brinkerhoff, 'Assessing and Improving Partnership Relationships and Outcomes: A Proposed Framework', *Evaluation and Program Planning* 25.3 (August 2002): 215–31, and also Ken Caplan, Joe Gomme, Josses Mugabi and Leda Stott, *Assessing Partnership Performance: Understanding the Drivers for Success* (London: Building Partnerships for Development in Water and Sanitation, 2007; www.bpdws.org).

11   See 'The PGA Framework: Promoting Best Practice in the Management of Partnerships for Sustainable Development' developed by AccountAbility and available at www.pgaframework.org.

12   IBLF, *Talking the Walk: A Communication Manual for Partnership Practitioners* (London: The Partnering Initiative, IBLF, 2008).

13   See Sarah Earl, Fred Carden and Terry Smutylo, *Outcome Mapping: Building Learning and Reflection into Development Programs* (Ottawa, Canada: International Development Research Centre [IDRC], 2001; www.idrc.ca) and UN Development Programme, UN Institute for Training and Research, UN Office for Partnerships and UN Global Compact Office, *Enhancing Partnership Value: A Tool for Assessing Sustainability and Impact* (New York: United Nations Global Compact Office, 2007).

14   Ros Tennyson and Rafal Serafin, *Getting Better: Proving and Improving the Value of Cross-sector Partnerships* (Working Paper for the development of a new toolbook; London: The Partnering Initiative, IBLF, 2009).

or how contexts have changed during the activity that might make those objectives inappropriate in the future. For instance, as the scale and depth of challenges such as climate change become more apparent, the level of ambition embodied by existing partnership objectives may have to rise. To reassess objectives effectively requires reflection on the values that gave rise to those objectives. The means of achieving those objectives also needs assessment in light of those values.

During any evaluation, it is important to map out the elements of any activity that is being assessed. The typical elements of any evaluation are summarised in **Box 15**. Done well, evaluation can be a tool for progressive transformation. Evaluations that give equal focus to the appropriateness of an activity, as to its effectiveness and efficiency, that draw upon multiple types and sources of information, seek to empower all participants with new insights, and feed into strategic planning, are worth the expense of time and effort to do well.

It is crucial for such evaluations to involve collective processes bringing together participants to co-evaluate an activity, with a professional evaluator facilitating this process, rather than simply interviewing participants and writing a report. Therefore, in this guidebook I offer a couple of exercises which I recommend you do with colleagues involved in a particular partnership. The first is a simple SWOT analysis of strengths, weaknesses, opportunities and threats of/to the partnership (**Box 16**). This is a useful process to consider the partnership as a whole rather than one's own organisation, to consider limitations as well as benefits of existing partnerships, and to consider future trends that could impact the partnership and its appropriateness.

Box 15 **Typical evaluation approaches**

The elements of any activity that can be evaluated include the values that motivate an activity, the needs addressed by the activity, and the objectives, inputs, processes, outputs and outcomes of that activity.

- Values refer to the principles of behaviour that arise out of assumptions, feelings, knowledge or beliefs, and are tacitly or explicit agreed to by a group of people engaged in an activity
- Needs are the societal challenges that are being addressed by the activity
- Objectives or goals are the specific aims that have been defined at the outset of the activity to solve some of the needs
- Inputs are the financial, physical and human resources that are allocated and consumed to enable an activity
- Processes are the operations of the activity being evaluated, such as a project started by a partnership, or its governance processes, or the whole suite of processes involve in the partnership as a whole
- Outputs are the products or immediate results created by the activity
- Outcomes are the broader consequences for the participants, beneficiaries and wider society. The outcomes can be, but may not necessarily be, the impact of the outputs

Different forms of data can be collected for each of these elements, using quantitative or qualitative methods, drawn from different stakeholders in a partnership. With the growth of large donor-funded projects involving public-interest organisations, in recent times the increased requirement for evaluation has, ironically, had a mixed effect on impact. This is because processes of evaluation have focused too much on what can be counted, and what output can be directly related to one input. This reductionism and determinism can stifle innovation and more creative ways of seeking greater social change. It also can undermine the ability of an evaluation process to enable organisational learning and strategic planning.

Box 16 **Partnership SWOT (Exercise G)**

This exercise is designed to help you consider the state of the partnership as a whole rather than your own organisation, and to consider future trends that could impact the partnership and its appropriateness.

Either on your own, with a colleague or in a team, write down at least five strengths, five weaknesses, five opportunities and five threats to your chosen partnership. If you are in a team, using different colours of sticky notes for each category and placing these on a wall can help with effective sharing and grouping of ideas from the team.

- **Strength** (resources or capacities the partnership is using effectively to achieve its objectives):

_____
_____
_____
_____
_____
....
....

- **Weakness** (limitations or problems in the partnership that is keeping it from achieving its objectives):

_____
_____
_____
_____
_____
....
....

- **Opportunity** (favourable changes or trends in the context of the partnership that may enhance its ability to achieve its objectives):

_____
_____
_____
_____
_____

....

....

- **Threats** (unfavourable changes or trends in the context of the partnership that may damage its ability to achieve its objectives):

_____

_____

_____

_____

_____

....

....

- Having written an initial five ideas for each, look at whether they relate to the dimensions of effectiveness, efficiency or appropriateness of the partnership. If one of these dimensions is not addressed yet by what you wrote, try to identify an idea for that. If doing this in a team, discuss which dimensions are not represented and identify some together
- Next, try to see how a particular strength or opportunity could actually be regarded as a weakness or a threat, and how a weakness or a threat could actually be regarded as a strength or an opportunity. If so, what is critical in making something positive for the partnership? Alter some of your entries if you need to as a result of that thinking
- Identify which strengths can help you take advantage or which opportunities, and connect them with lines
- What could you do differently, or with more effort, to employ your strengths to develop the opportunities?
- Consider which weaknesses and threats are critical, and how they could be addressed. Then identify which of those actions will reduce the strengths and opportunities the least
- What could you do differently, or with more effort, to ward off the threats or compensate for weaknesses without undermining your strengths and opportunities?

Partnerships involve expanding one's connections with other organisations and thus one's awareness of those organisations, in order to effectively share resources, risks and rewards. Therefore, an evaluation framework for partnering can reflect the importance of that process of expanding awareness and connection. The latest evolutionary science provides a reminder of how the success of an individual is co-dependent on the success of the groups and wider systems within which the individual exists. We therefore use the latest evolutionary view of individual 'fitness' as a framework for partnership evaluation.

'Fitness' in evolutionary theory describes the capability of an individual to enable its genes to continue to exist in future generations. The organism's ability to reproduce is part of its fitness, and is often assumed to describe the totality of its fitness. However, the ability of the community that an organism exists within (such as a flock or herd) to reproduce as a whole, and the ability of the ecosystem that community exists within to sustain itself over time, are also aspects of the individual organism's 'total' fitness. This is because natural selection works not only at the level of individual organisms but also at the levels of population and ecosystem. These insights come from some of the latest evolutionary biology on issues such as 'extended phenotypes', 'multi-level' or group selection and 'universal fitness'. This suggests that 'survival of the fittest' can no longer be understood as the survival of the individuals most able to compete with other individuals, but as the survival of individuals both competing and cooperating effectively within a population that in turn competes and cooperates within an ecosystem that it does not harm.

'Inclusive fitness' is a concept popularised by biologist Richard Dawkins, who identified how certain social behaviours may help gene codes survive but not a particular individual, such as instances of altruism in nature as shown by the Belding ground squirrel.[15] He argued that fitness includes both individual fitness and the fitness of its group. He further developed this argument with the notion of an extended phenotype, whereby structures emerging from patterns of interaction between individuals, such as termite mounds, bee hives and coral reefs, are as much expressions of genes as individual phenotypes. They become successful structures of interaction because they benefit the replication of the genes that determined them. Others have stressed the importance of understanding that natural selection is multi-level, working at the level of groups like flocks, as well as at the level

15 Richard Dawkins, *The Selfish Gene* (Oxford, UK: Oxford University Press, 1976).

of individuals with a group.[16] In addition to inclusive fitness, the fitness of a whole ecosystem is important to the fitness of an individual. This is recognised by ecologists who write about 'ecosystem fitness', such as the fitness of a river ecosystem. With no river, there are no fish, no matter how fit those fish are at an individual or shoal level. However, as far as I am aware, this concept has not yet been employed to describe a dimension of the fitness of an individual organism in an ecosystem like a river. Instead, that idea has been explored in epidemiology; for example, the term 'universal fitness' is used to describe the way a parasite's fitness is not benefited by causing the host to die quickly, as there is less time for its transmission to other hosts. If an organism kills the life-supporting environment, then it kills itself.[17] I provide some of the scientific theories and references here to refute the popular mainstream notion of 'survival of the fittest' which is based on the state of evolutionary science over 30 years ago. However, it is important to note that I am not suggesting organisational behaviour can be explained by evolutionary science, but that it provides a useful metaphor and model for evaluation and strategy.

When used to understand organisational performance, the concept of fitness invites us expand our horizons of time and space, considering how ready the organisation is for the future, and how it interacts positively with its surrounding environment, in comparison to other organisations.[18] Transposing from the fitness of organisms, organisational fitness can be understood as comprising the following three levels:

---

16 Samuel Bowles, 'Group Competition, Reproductive Leveling, and the Evolution of Human Altruism', *Science* 314.5805 (2006): 1,569–72 (www.sciencemag.org/cgi/content/full/314/5805/1569).

17 Gráinne H. Long, Brian H.K. Chan, Judith E. Allen, Andrew F. Read and Andrea L. Graham, 'Experimental Manipulation of Immune-Mediated Disease and its Fitness Costs for Rodent Malaria Parasites,' *BMC Evolutionary Biology* 8 (2008): 128 (www.ncbi.nlm.nih.gov/pubmed/18447949).

18 There are differing views on whether direct fitness is best understood as a quality of an organism, its genotype or a particular gene. However, as fitness describes the sustaining of particular genes, some suggest that it is useful to extend the metaphor to consider an organisation's DNA as the routines and capabilities within an organisation that maintain it. In this partnership evaluation framework, I apply the concept of fitness in a general way to organisational partners, and the partnerships, as well as the routines and capabilities of partnering. I use the term 'processes' rather than 'routines', popular in some management theory, due to it being more readily understood by practitioners. Further work is required to explore how useful the concept is for assessing the fitness of specific partnering routines/processes and capabilities.

- **Direct organisational fitness**. The relative ability of an individual organisation, or its particular processes and capabilities, to prosper in accordance with its mission, through its ability to secure resources and exchange information within a community of other organisations

- **Inclusive organisational fitness**. The relative ability of an individual organisation, or its particular processes and capabilities, to prosper in accordance with its mission, not only through its direct fitness but also by benefiting the fitness of the community within which it exists

- **Universal organisational fitness**. The relative ability of an individual organisation, or its particular processes and capabilities, to prosper in accordance with its mission, not only through its direct fitness and inclusive fitness, but also through benefiting the universe of life that the organisation and its community exist within[19]

This organisational fitness framework (OFF) highlights how an organisation's success is co-dependent on how it benefits not only its intended beneficiaries and stakeholders, but also wider society and the natural environment. It encourages us to consider the 'me', 'we' and 'all of us' dimensions to organisational life. Applying this framework to the process of partnering highlights how a partnership can be evaluated by its costs and benefits to the partnering organisation and its beneficiaries (direct partner fitness), to all participants in that partnership (inclusive partner fitness) and to society as a whole (universal partner fitness).[20] Thus a partnership fitness framework can be outlined and used to plan an evaluation of a partnership, from

---

19   Note the emphasis on the relative ability of an organisation, as evolution reminds us that it is the relative ability of an individual, population or ecosystem to succeed that determines whether its characteristics (genes and corresponding phenotypes) will spread. Note also that I provide for an emphasis on either the organisation or its particular processes and capabilities as the item that succeeds, given that some consider organisational routines to be the organisational equivalent of genes and thus a better focus for an evolutionary lens on organisations.

20   In this model, I do not identify the assessment of benefit for a partnership's intended beneficiaries as a separate step, as I see them as central to the assessment of how a partnership benefits an organisation, given that organisations are meant to be run for their beneficiaries. Unfortunately this is often not the case, as the interests of the managers of an organisation may predominate.

the perspective of how it benefits the direct, inclusive and universal fitness of an individual partner (**Diagram V**).[21]

Diagram V **The partnership fitness framework**

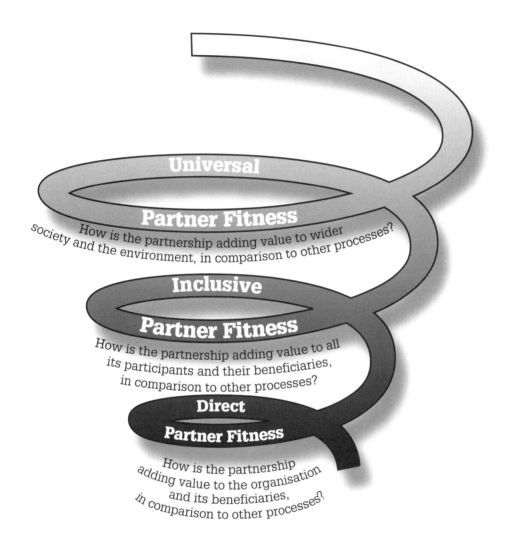

---

21 This organisational fitness framework can be used for any organisational form or routine. Thus, rather than being applied to the individual partner organisation, with its partnering competence and routine, it could be applied to a partnership as a whole. This would entail considering: (a) direct partnership fitness as the relative ability of the partnership to deliver for its participants and secure resources to continue; (b) inclusive partnership fitness as the relative ability of the partnership to benefit its stakeholders and other similar partnerships while also doing 'a'; (c) universal partnership fitness as the relative ability of the partnership to benefit the wider society and ecosystem it exists within, as well as doing 'a' and 'b'.

If you want to map out how to evaluate your partnering in a way that recognises the co-dependence of your organisation on wider systems, then you can use **Exercise H** in **Box 17** to begin. It incorporates the main dimensions of evaluation (effectiveness, efficiency and appropriateness) with the main components of evaluation (values, needs, inputs, processes, outputs, outcomes), within the three levels of the organisational fitness framework. The framework may appear abstract at first, but guides you towards mapping out how you can generate information to assess all levels of fitness. Topics arising during an assessment of direct partner fitness include how the views of intended beneficiaries influence the partnership, or how to quantify the full resources being invested in the partnership. Topics arising through an assessment of inclusive partner fitness include the need to check all partners are delivering on their pre-agreed commitments, and how to optimise the partnership's management and governance. Issues that can arise during an assessment of universal partner fitness include how the partnership is strengthening and not disenfranchising the public sector. However, the exact focus and content of an evaluation will depend on which generation of partnering your organisation is involved in, as the outputs and outcomes of second- and third-generation partnerships are less easily quantified and related to specific inputs and processes. For them, the latest approaches to evaluating advocacy are important.[22] The flexibility of the framework is intentional, as over-prescriptive evaluations can stifle innovation and learning. Just as variation is key to effective evolution in nature, variations in organisational processes will be essential to the successful evolution of partnerships.

---

22 For the latest information on evaluation, visit the Monitoring and Evaluation Network at www.mande.co.uk and the Innovation Network at www.innonet.org. Information on evaluating advocacy is at www.innonet.org/index.php?section_id=101&content_id=633.

Box 17 **Developing a plan for evaluating partner fitness (Exercise H)**

This exercise is designed to enable you to design an evaluation process that will generate information relevant to assessing your organisation's ability to be an effective partner – for itself, its partners and wider society.

Work through the following questions on a separate piece of paper, individually or in a team.

A Orientation

- What is the purpose of this evaluation?
- Who will decide on the conclusions of the evaluation, and the follow-up actions?
- Are there resources and organisational commitment to a process for achieving these evaluation goals?

B Data identification

- What were the needs that the partnership sought to address, in terms of the beneficiaries, the organisation, the other partners, and wider society and environment?
- What were the objectives that the partnership established to meet those needs, in terms of the beneficiaries, the organisation, the other partners, and wider society and environment?
- What values gave rise to a commitment to work on the needs in the way specified by the objectives?
- What types of input can you identify, and how will you collect data on them?
- What types of process can you identify, and how will you collect data on them?
- What types and sources of information could you seek to identify outputs, and which are practicable?
- What types and sources of information could you seek to identify outcomes, and which are practicable?

Once you have decided how you will generate information on outputs and outcomes, then you can start assessing partner fitness.

C Assessing direct partner fitness

Effectiveness

- How will you assess positive impact of the partnership on your organisation and its beneficiaries?
- How will you compare these impacts with the experiences of other partnerships?

→

- How will you compare these impacts with the experiences of other non-partnership activities to effect similar social changes?

Efficiency

- How will you assess the costs of the partnership or any negative side effects, to your organisation and its beneficiaries?
- How will you compare these costs and side effects with the experiences of other partnerships?
- How will you compare these costs and side effects with the experiences of other non-partnership activities to effect similar social changes?

Appropriateness

- How will you assess the partnership's effect on the legitimacy of your organisation and the claims of your beneficiaries?
- How will you assess trends in the changing context of your organisation and beneficiaries to understand the future suitability of the partnership?
- How will you ascertain how similar organisations to yours are assessing the appropriateness of their activities on similar issues?

D Assessing inclusive partner fitness

Effectiveness

- How will you assess the positive impact of the partnership on all other organisational partners and their beneficiaries?
- How will you encourage those other partners to benchmark their experience with the partnership in comparison to other partnerships and non-partnering activities, in order to advise you on relative performance?

Efficiency

- How will you assess the costs of the partnership or any negative side effects, to all other partner organisations and their beneficiaries?
- How will you encourage those other partners to benchmark those costs or negative side effects in comparison to other partnerships and non-partnering activities, in order to advise you on relative performance?

Appropriateness

- How will you assess trends in the changing context of all other partners and their beneficiaries to understand the future suitability of the partnership?
- How will you encourage those other partners to assess the appropriateness of the partnership in order to advise you on this aspect of the partnership's worth?

E Assessing universal partner fitness

Effectiveness

- How will you assess the positive impact of the partnership on other stakeholders and wider society?
- How will you compare these impacts with the experiences of other partnerships?
- How will you compare these impacts with the experiences of other non-partnership activities to effect similar social changes?

Efficiency

- How will you assess the costs of the partnership or any negative side effects, to other stakeholders and wider society?
- How will you compare these costs and possible side effects with the experiences of other partnerships?
- How will you compare these costs and possible side effects with the experiences of other non-partnership activities done to effect similar social changes?

Appropriateness

- How will you assess the extent to which the partnership is contributing to a universal solution to the needs it seeks to address?
- How will you assess the extent to which all the partnership's operations are consistent with the values that gave rise to your organisation's participation in it?
- How will you ascertain how similar organisations to yours are assessing the appropriateness of their activities on similar issues?

Evolution helps us understand some dynamics of how units interact and thrive. I am not suggested that Darwinian evolution is actually taking place at an organisational level, but that it is a useful metaphor and framework for thinking about interconnectedness, interdependence, competition and change. The evaluation framework does not comprise an evolutionary theory of organisational behaviour. However, it is an explanatory model that can predict some behaviours. Organisations that intuitively or explicitly attend to the three aspects of their fitness will:

- Begin working at larger scales of interaction and impact
- Create greater social change, encounter less criticism from intended beneficiaries and generate fewer unintended consequences, if acting with good intention
- Create new institutions out of their collaborations that will have greater social impacts than, and outlast, the parent organisations

Box 18 **Evolutionary theory, the organisation and social change**

There are three areas of study that apply evolutionary concepts to society: evolutionary psychology, evolutionary theory in management, and memetics. Evolutionary psychology is not relevant here as I am not seeking to predict personal behaviour, and few people agree that all social behaviours can be usefully explained through genetically determined individual preferences.

Evolutionary theory in management has focused on what might be usefully considered the equivalent of DNA for an organisation, with organisational routines or procedures being the favoured concept. As such the market is seen to select for or against these routines, through acting on the organism, which is considered to be the organisation. This literal application stumbles when one considers how variation in routines occurs, especially given that changes in routines are often directly intentional, not random mutations. The actual application of these ideas in advising management appears very limited.

Memetics is an attempt to directly apply the conceptual framework of genetics to society, without relying on genes as the only information carriers that demonstrate self-replicating behaviours. It is a way of suggesting that ideas and their physical embodiment (such as a piece of architecture) in society act in similar ways to genes in nature, and spread in similar ways. The writer Susan Blackmore has suggested that these information patterns or memes are not simply human creations but have a life of their own and humans are mere agents for the replication of these memes; patterns of information in society shape our interaction with them in ways that lead to the reproduction of those patterns, and the gradual changing of those patterns. This theory suggests that, for example, we exist for housing, rather than housing existing for us. Many scientists and philosophers reject this notion outright, as do many lay people. It is an interesting but largely unhelpful and distracting application of evolutionary concepts. Instead, information patterns in both the natural world and society can be understood to exist in dialectic relationship with individual organisms. The latest science, for instance quantum mechanics, provides some evidence for the concept of an 'akashic record' that stores all information patterns that ever existed in a field that transcends time and space of our known dimensions, yet influences the ease with which future information patterns may emerge. Several authors, including Ervin László and Margaret Wheatley,[a] explore the potential for scientific theories such as evolution to be more literally applied to organisational strategy and behaviour, or social change, than is done in this guidebook.

a See Ervin László, *Science and the Akashic Field: An Integral Theory of Everything.* (Rochester, VT: Inner Traditions, 2004), and Margaret Wheatley, *Leadership and the New Science: Learning about Organisations from Orderly Universe* (San Francisco: Berrett Koehler, 1992).

5 Evolving to the next generation of partnership

All societal partnerships are evaluated to some extent, whether by the participants, in a systematic or ad hoc way, or by external groups, including critics. As a result some of the limitations of first-generation forms of partnership are perceived by participants, and some seek to address them by evolving the partnership to a new level.

If you want to evolve a first-generation partnership, then it is important to:

- Refine your understanding of how the business partner's core operations relate to the issues your existing partnership or organisation is focused on

- Assess whether a company's level of strategic commitment to corporate responsibility allows it to work effectively on such an agenda

- Clarify how your organisation can improve its readiness to be an effective partner

- Explore with a company the various interests it has in relation to the agenda on which you want to work with it

If this is relevant to your situation, I recommend the exercise in **Box 19**. Otherwise, skip forward to the next section. The exercise includes the option of a role-play, if you are able to work through this guidebook with a colleague or in a team. The role-play focuses on how you could start a conversation with an existing corporate partner about evolving the current partnership to the second generation. Issues that can emerge during such a discussion include:

- The limited understanding by public-interest organisation staff of the corporate partner, including its strategy, business model and decision-making processes, and thus the need to obtain more information, perhaps through staff exchanges or more prolonged and open-ended interactions than usual

- That corporations have a myriad of interests, including commercial near term and long term, seeking to ensure the public-interest organisation continues to gain some benefit from the relationship, and the personal concerns of business people for the social and environmental challenges the partnership addresses. All these areas can be worked on

- A limited understanding of how the public-interest organisation can offer value as a partner on process, product, standards or exchange partnerships, and thus a need to clarify its relevant skills, capacities and networks and how it can enhance those

These exercises were used in a strategy workshop with the private-sector team in CARE International UK. Since then the private-sector team has sought to work more with companies to improve their operations to promote social change in line with the organisation's mandate. 'In the tea sector in Sri Lanka, we have collaborated with the Ethical Tea Partnership as part of a European Commission funded programme to support tea estate workers through the creation of community development forums (CDFs)', explains CARE International's Tim Bishop.

> With the ETP we've used CDFs to: support the improvement in manager–worker relationships; promote gender empowerment (through the establishment of female supervisors in estates historically run by men); positively address social issues such as alcohol misuse; and also evidenced, in some cases, an increase in estate productivity of tea at the same time.[1]

---

1   Personal communication with the author, July 2010.

Box 19 **Evolving to the second generation (Exercise I)**

The exercise is designed to help you evolve your existing partnerships from a first- to a second-generation orientation. The exercise has two parts: the first can be done by oneself, the second requires a colleague or team.

Scoping the potential

Reflect on or discuss with a colleague the following questions, making notes on a separate piece of paper:

- Does the level of the public-interest organisation's overall approach to business and the market need to evolve in order to explore second-generation partnerships, and if so, what or who can drive such change? Refer to the diagram you drew in **Exercise F**, **Box 14**.
- How does the company directly impact on the people or issues of concern to the partnership (and the public-interest organisation), through their internal business operations, including supply chain and customers?
- Is the company working on these issues?
- If no, what needs to change in the company or in its operating environment to address the reasons for inaction?
- Does the public-interest organisation have any networks, competencies or capacities to help the company change its internal performance, or drive changes in the operating environment, on these issues?
- What more could the public-interest organisation learn about its own performance, such as effectiveness and efficiency, through further engagement with the company?
- How might you start a conversation with your partner about moving to the second generation?
- If the current corporate partner is being held back from a higher level of engagement, what types of company might not have those restrictions?

Role-play on evolving the partnership

Ideally create a group of equal numbers of representatives of your public-interest organisation and a company that you partner, with the role-players all having some knowledge of the current partnership and corporate partner. Then follow this process:

- The public-interest organisation representatives discuss how the company directly impacts on the people or issues of concern to the partnership, through their internal business operations, and therefore what might be a good idea for a second-generation partnership. For example, focusing on product development and marketing, a new management process, a new standards system, a staff exchange scheme, or perhaps a mix of them all or something altogether different

- The public-interest organisation representatives then begin a conversation with the people playing the company, seeking to gain commitment to launch a second-generation partnership. The conversation could cover at least three areas of corporate interest, including commercial (either near term and long term; contingent on where the company is on pyramid of responsible enterprise strategies), political (such as concern that the public-interest organisation and other stakeholders continue to feel positive about the partnership), and personal interests (the individual commitment of business people to social and environmental challenges addressed by the partnership)

- The public-interest organisation staff seek agreement from the company on an agenda for a follow-up meeting

- After the role-play, everyone notes down the arguments that seemed to make sense, and any new information that is needed to exemplify these arguments that you may use in future

Evolving to third-generation partnerships

Second-generation societal partnerships have played a key role in advancing corporate responsibility. Standards development partnerships, in particular, have helped link responsible consumers, whether individuals or institutions, to socially and environmentally more advanced producers and suppliers. Consequently their influence has extended beyond the initial partners and has begun to shift markets as a whole, leading to some claiming they represent a 'certification revolution'.[2] However, as discussed earlier, there are limits to corporate social and environmental performance within existing market frameworks (see **Box 8**). Consequently a responsible company should be adopting a strategy of societal leadership, to help shift the market frameworks to enable it to operate profitably through social and

---

2   Michael E. Conroy, *Branded! How the 'Certification Revolution' is Transforming Global Corporations* (Gabriola Island, Canada: New Society Publishers, 2007).

environmental excellence. Dennis Pamlin of WWF Sweden argues for NGOs to 'separate the companies in the West that belong to the three different generations' in order to target those that can collaborate on more transformative agendas.[3]

Evidence from the World Economic Forum (WEF) indicates that many companies are aware of how systemic social and environmental challenges impact on their future financial performance. 'Investing in a sound and secure operating environment' was third highest in a list of reasons for partnering identified by respondents to a WEF survey, with over 40% indicating this challenge as a motivation for partnering with public-interest organisations. A key systemic challenge that WEF is working on is corruption, which the World Bank estimates involves about US$1 trillion being spent on bribes each year – some 3% of global GDP.[4]

There are companies that regard their corporate responsibility work as a smokescreen for increasing corporate control of resources in ways that undermine sustainability and social justice, and critics point to the way such companies use lobbying and advertising to undermine progress to a more sustainable and just world economy.

On corporate lobbying, one professor at the London School of Economics has documented that corporations 'work, quite deliberately and often rather covertly, as political actors, and often have direct access to those at the highest levels of formal political and administrative power with considerable success'.[5] Australian political scientists have demonstrated how corporations and their lobbying groups are able to manoeuvre on the international scene in order to generate the rules they want, and undermine those they perceive as problematic, being particularly critical of the role of pharmaceutical companies on intellectual property and access to medicines.[6] Campaign finance is a particular challenge. The 2008 US election was the most expensive ever, with over a billion dollars spent in the process. An increasing amount of this money came from individuals and their associations, but corporations still contributed the majority, in order to influence the policies

3   Dennis Pamlin, 'From Philanthropy to Core Business: Opening a Window', *Sustainability Sweden* 1 (2006): 30–1.

4   WEF, *Partnering for Success: Business Perspectives on Multistakeholder Partnerships* (Geneva: WEF, 2005): 17.

5   Leslie Sklair, 'Debate Transnational Corporations: As Political Actors', *New Political Economy* 3 (1998): 284–7.

6   John Braithwaite and Peter Drahaus, *Global Business Regulation* (Cambridge, UK: Cambridge University Press: 2000).

of the candidates. The role of corporate campaign finance in influencing politicians' policy proposals is a challenge to democracy worldwide.[7]

Globally, corporations spend billions on advertising products and services. This content often focuses on creating desires to consume more, whether or not the products and services are socially or environmentally preferable to others, thereby driving up resource consumption and pollution at a time of resource scarcity and climate change.[8] The interests of advertisers also influences programme content. At the last count, 40% of all the world's media were controlled by five large transnational corporations.[9] Despite the endeavours of committed journalists, the corporate media have been demonstrated to filter the news, limiting its ability to communicate clearly and regularly the problems of our current economic system.[10] Moreover, media firms are managed to generate advertising revenue, which creates a pressure to quickly boost ratings, so people experience increasingly simple and inconsequential audio, print and television media.

Through these communications functions, companies shape the market frameworks that many business people now recognise do not help them to become a responsible enterprise. Consequently these communications functions need to be leveraged to create the appropriate market frameworks. Lobbying and advertising have, therefore, emerged as key dimensions to third-generation societal partnerships such as USCAP, mentioned earlier.

---

7   Greg Palast, *The Best Democracy That Money Can Buy: An Investigative Reporter Exposes the Truth About Globalisation, Corporate Cons, and High Finance Fraudsters* (London: Pluto Press, 2002).

8   Jules Peck and Anthony Kleanthous, *Let Them Eat Cake* (Godalming, UK: WWF-UK, 2006).

9   Andrew Simms, Tom Bigg and Nick Robins, *It's Democracy Stupid: The Trouble With the Global Economy – The United Nations' Lost Role and Democratic Reform of the IMF, World Bank and the World Trade Organization* (London: New Economics Foundation, 2000).

10   This is described in Edward S. Hernan and Noam Chomsky, *Manufacturing Consent: The Political Economy of the Mass Media* (London: Vintage, 1994). First, they identified how the business interests of the owner companies influence reporting. Second, media managers need to please (and certainly not upset) current and potential advertisers. Third, journalists often rely on press releases from organisations with a commercial interest in influencing the media. This reliance is increased as profit objectives regulate the amount of time most journalists have for research. Consequently many media outlets peddle the views of organisations which falsely claim expertise in order to promote a political agenda. Fourth, journalists who rock the boat are liable to professional criticism and sometimes litigation. A fifth filter is a blind acceptance of neoliberal economic ideology, so that many journalists were bemused at, and uninterested in, fundamental critiques of the economic system.

Such partnerships focus not only on improvements within, and benefits to, the participants, but also on changing the barriers and drivers that constitute their operational contexts and those of equivalent non-participants, so that the impact of the partnership is both deep and broad enough to address the societal challenges involved. Characteristics of these partnerships are that they go:

- **Broader**. Broader participation, by involving a wider range of organisations in society, and broader purpose, by seeking to influence not only the participants but also non-participating organisations, and to have an impact on a broader range of behaviours affecting a broader range of social and environmental issues

- **Deeper**. Deeper systems, by working on the underlying drivers that create unsustainable behaviours, and deeper self, by engendering the necessary level of personal awareness and commitment to be part of a complex and challenging effort

Key steps in a process of moving towards more transformative partnerships include:

- Recognising the limitations of existing partnerships and partnering in general

- Taking collective and personal responsibility for the systems that create those limitations

- Valuing the potential of relations across sectors with corporations that strongly shape those systems

- Assessing the nature of those systems and the ways that companies shape them

- Understanding the various reasons why corporate partners and persons might seek to work on these forms of corporate influences

- Envisioning the type of market or societal system transformation you seek, and the type of system you could generate through a partnership to achieve this wider transformation

Each of these steps needs to occur with corporate partners, for reasons of both information generation on issues that may be beyond the knowledge of your organisation, and in order to encourage or affirm shifts in thinking from your corporate partners. However, it is also important for your organisation to better understand its own current assessment of partnership performance and systemic change of markets and societies.

It is one thing to recognise the need for more systemic change and another to know what actions that implies. There is a need for all of us concerned with systemic social changes to become smarter about what that entails. The Action Town project summarises the challenge well, focusing on environmental public-interest organisations:

> [NGOs] have well-developed skills in analyzing and assessing environmental problems, but often lack knowledge and capacity on how to effectively resolve them in terms of understanding the complex functioning of the economic and social systems within which both the problem and the potential solutions exist. On the other hand, academia has long experience in these related areas, but are seldom involved in actively creating and promoting solutions, as well as being somewhat isolated from civil society organizations. What seem to be missing are the capacities and the mechanisms of joining these knowledge areas in order to design tools that can successfully resolve these environmental crises.[11]

Therefore, to become more proficient in evolving collaborations to effect systemic change, public-interest organisations need to learn from various academic theories on social change. That is a complicated challenge, as there are at least five broad intellectual disciplines within which people inquire into how change happens: economic, social and political studies; business, organisation and management studies; natural sciences; art and design studies; and religious, spiritual and philosophical studies. Within the field of partnering and sustainability only two of these intellectual areas are being widely discussed as providing tools for social change. The leading intellectual area is business, organisation and management studies, which is not surprising, given that it is most easily connected to the realities of managers. Consequently much focus is on how entrepreneurship drives system disruption, how social marketing can influence publics, how networks can help organise people, and how organisational development frameworks such as 'soft systems' can help with planning change. There is a strong emphasis on group processes as mechanisms of social change, with process tools including Appreciative Inquiry, Dynamic Facilitation, Future Search,

---

11 Burcu Tunçer, Pamela Ragazzi and Michael Narberhaus, *Better and New NGO Strategies to Tackle the Sustainable Consumption and Production Challenge? Roadmapping ...* (Discussion Paper for Action Town; Wuppertal: UNEP/Wuppertal and WWF, 6 February 2009).

Open Space Technology, Scenario Thinking, World Café and the U-process.[12] The ELIAS project, mentioned earlier, addresses social change from this organisation studies background, and integrates a variety of techniques into what it calls 'presencing'. In recent years the art and design studies field has become more active in the social change space, with 'design thinking' becoming popular in some circles. Developing new processes that combine the creativity of 'design thinking' with insights from relevant social sciences on social and behavioural change is the key challenge for professional facilitators of collaborative action in the coming years.[13]

One area where insights from different disciplines are being integrated to enhance understanding of social change is social psychology. This field blends insights from psychology, semiology and critical discourse analysis, to explain how assumptions are shaped and in turn shape our behaviour. This field became popular in the mid noughties in the US among political movements that opposed the administration of George W. Bush.[14] Since then the role of 'cognitive framing' and personal identity has been discussed by NGOs seeking to influence behaviours and policies,[15] as well as in the field of CSR.[16] However, I am not aware of how it has been mobilised in the development of cross-sector partnerships.

As more people become interested in how to collaborate for social change and create third-generation partnerships, so the insights from different intellectual disciplines will, it is hoped, blend. Sometimes the same ideas even emerge in different disciplines: for instance, sustainability management consultant and entrepreneur John Elkington has developed a social change mapping matrix which is a mirror image of philosopher Ken Wilbur's four-quadrant model.[17]

---

12 For more information on these techniques see www.socialinnovator.info/process-social-innovation and patternsofchange.wordpress.com.

13 Jem Bendell, 'Will Design Thinking Save Us?' Lifeworth Consulting Blog, 2010; www.lifeworth.com/consult/2010/05/will-design-thinking-save-us-the-creativity-revolution-in-responsible-business.

14 George Lakoff, *Don't Think of an Elephant: Know Your Values and Frame the Debate* (White River Junction, VT: Chelsea Green Publishing, 2006).

15 Tom Crompton, *Weathercocks and Signposts: The Environment Movement at a Cross Roads* (Godalming, UK: WWF-UK, 2008).

16 J. Bendell *et al.*, *Tipping Frames: The Lifeworth Annual Review of Corporate Responsibility 2006* (2007; Lifeworth; www.lifeworth.net).

17 See John Elkington, 'A New Paradigm for Change', *What Matters*, 6 April 2010; whatmatters.mckinseydigital.com/social_entrepreneurs/a-new-paradigm-for-change, and Ken Wilber, *A Theory of Everything: An Integral Vision for Business, Politics, Science and Spirituality* (Shambhala Publications, 2000).

One of the broadest disciplines that is highly relevant to social change has not been used widely to inform strategic planning in existing cross-sector partnerships. That is economic, social and political studies, which hosts fields of inquiry such as the sociology of power, social movements theory and neo-institutional theory. These theories focus on large-scale social change. Unfortunately the insight from these fields is somewhat trapped in the respective academic jargon and theoretical preoccupations of academia. Elsewhere I have made attempts to apply social movements theories to responsible business,[18] and network thinking to NGO campaigns on responsible business and economic governance.[19] In this guidebook I seek to enable the development of third-generation partnerships by providing a model that distils some of the insights from neo-institutional theory. This model outlines four main processes of interpersonal relations that constitute social systems, including markets (**Box 20**).[20] The model emphasises how interpersonal processes of believing, assuming, regulating and resourcing continually reconstitute social systems. These processes interact with each other and are summarised in **Diagram VI**.

18 Jem Bendell (ed.), *The Corporate Responsibility Movement: Five Years of Global Corporate Responsibility Analysis from Lifeworth, 2001–2005* (Sheffield, UK: Greenleaf Publishing, 2009; www.greenleaf-publishing.com/crmovement).

19 Jem Bendell and Annekathrin Ellersiek, *Noble Networks? Advocacy for Global Justice and the 'Network Effect'* (Geneva: UNRISD, 2009).

20 This model is a synthesis and simplification of insights from structuration theory and institutional theory. The term 'market' could be replaced by 'social', given that this model is also useful in describing societal change, i.e. social factors and social actors.

Box 20 **Interpersonal processes that create social systems**

By integrating and simplifying sociological studies, four main processes of interpersonal relations that constitute social systems, including markets, can be identified. These are:

- **Processes of believing**. Where people participate in processes of believing in something, including the physical manifestations (and thus facilitators) of this process, covering such things as social norms, beliefs, values, aspirations or social obligations. Often professed or expected by influential members of a particular subsystem (for example, formal associations of organisations and professions, networks of individuals and firms) as 'what ought to be', inviting people to do the 'right' thing and adopt 'best practices' on a particular issue

- **Processes of assuming**. Where people participate in processes of assuming 'the way things are', and the way they are not, including the physical manifestations (and thus facilitators) of this process, involving such things as cognitive frames, interpretive schemes, discursive practices, prejudices, narratives and taken-for-granted assumptions, relating to themselves, others, society and the world. Habits can be understood here as embodied assumptions, i.e. physically practised ones

- **Processes of regulating**. Where people participate in processes of regulating human behaviour, including the material outputs and facilitators of this process, which may include regulations, governance systems, contracts and membership guidelines that primarily exert 'coercive' influences on organisations, pressurising them to conform to those demands, or otherwise face the threat of sanctions

- **Processes of resourcing**. Where people participate in processes affecting the resourcing of human behaviour, which may include finance, technology and manufactured goods, and natural environmental assets such as clean air and water. This also includes the soft resources of personal skills

Unlike some sociological studies within institutional theory, this model includes resources, thereby enabling us to appreciate how resource allocations influence processes of assuming, believing and regulating, and vice versa.[a] →

a The emphasis in this model is on the interpersonal. Processes of assuming, believing and resourcing can occur without it appearing that an individual is relating to others, or through interaction between one person and their environment. For example, one day you could wake up, see the sun rising over mountains, and have an epiphany which leads you to decide to cherish the environment and people much more. This

→

Some people group together various processes of assuming, believing, regulating and resourcing as 'structures'. To some this implies that there is an underlying factor, or process, that leads to emergent realities in a society, while others emphasise how these underlying factors or structures do not have a life separate to humans, and they are dependent on our participation in them to make them real. Structures can be regarded as groupings of mutually reinforcing interpersonal processes which are decisive in generating subsequent interpersonal processes that reinforce those initial interpersonal processes, and which create complex emergent properties in interpersonal systems. Capitalism, patriarchy and Western imperialism are examples of such 'structures'.

Considering the concept of patriarchy can illustrate this way of understanding structure and interpersonal systems. People may be *assuming* that men and women look, talk and think in certain ways and not others, and do different things in society. Language may reinforce this, and even act at a subconscious level. People may be *believing* that it is good for men to strive for certain things, and not women, who should aspire to other things. People may be *regulating* the actions of men and women, through organisational rules or national laws, in ways which reflect and reinforce assumptions and beliefs. People may be *resourcing* men and not women, or people showing certain attributes and not others, in terms of pay, promotions, skills training and working conditions. People may also be resourcing certain processes of assuming, believing and regulating, and not others, knowingly or not, thereby reinforcing the other processes of interpersonal relations.

---

is still interpersonal, in a number of ways. First, the context within which the experience arose – the state of the environment, the state of the person, the language used to interpret the emotion, and so on. Second, as you act with this new understanding you would interact with others directly, as well as indirectly through how you impact on our shared environment.

Diagram VI **Interpersonal processes that create social systems**

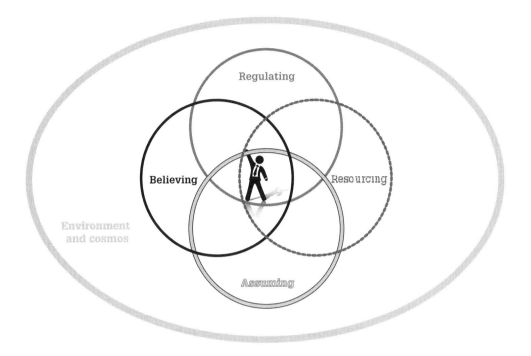

The model of what 'is' in society can be applied to markets, which are subsystems of society, and reveal the following key constituents of any market system:

- **Rules** governing markets come from local and national governments, intergovernmental bodies, industry and professional associations (regulating)

- **Norms** are practices that have become routine assumptions about behaviour (assuming)

- **Values** are what people believe is right or what they desire for themselves, and shifts in values shape consumer demand, trading relations, and employment (believing)

- New **technologies** continue to transform markets rapidly, the internet being an important example (resourcing)

- Changes in other **resources** such as oil, manufactured resources such as public infrastructure, and human resources such as population and settlements, collectively transform markets (resourcing)

Keeping this framework to hand may help ensure that you are considering various dimensions of the creation of societies and markets when you engage corporations. The exercise in **Box 21** employs this framework to help you begin thinking through how to evolve your partnering.

As we widen our view to the operational environment of a corporate partner, and the processes of system creation, it is important to recognise the web of relations around a corporate partner, so that you can identify opportunities to bring influence to bear on the whole sector or market. For example, a luxury retailer might begin to understand its power in editing consumer choices through its choice of inventory, and in influencing consumer understandings of what is aspirational and luxurious in ways that could promote sustainable and responsible consumption. A company can impact on the issues that public-interest organisations work on through influence on other actors, in addition to their internal operations.

Box 21 **Beginning a journey to third-generation societal partnerships (Exercise J)**

This exercise seeks to help you evolve your existing partnerships to have a wider and more lasting impact on the problem you address.

Either on your own, with a colleague or in a team, choose a specific partnership you know about and then reflect on or discuss the following questions, and note down your insights on a separate piece of paper.

- Are there limitations with your current partnership in creating a large-scale impact? If so, what are these limitations?
- What are the reasons given by your corporate partner for being unable to go further or faster in delivering change?
- Which of these reasons concern the operational environment of the company (consumer awareness, staff awareness, government policy, suppliers, investors, competitors, etc.)?
- What are the ways the company participates in the creation of this operational environment, through its myriad communications functions (e.g. advertising, lobbying, investor relations), both directly and indirectly through intermediaries?

The following questions are to support you in exploring further this last issue, by examining the ways the companies participate in the interpersonal processes of social system creation (outlined in **Box 20**):

1 How does the corporate partner shape the market through processes of resourcing?

- Which of these processes are affected by the partnership?
- What could be the commercial reasons for the company to begin working together on those processes?
- What can our organisation bring to a collaboration on these wider processes?

2 How does the corporate partner shape the market through processes of believing?

- Which of these processes are affected by the partnership?
- What are the commercial reasons for the company to begin working together on those processes?
- What can our organisation bring to a collaboration on these wider processes?

3 How does the corporate partner shape the market through processes of assuming?

- Which of these processes are affected by the partnership?
- What are the commercial reasons for the company to begin working together on those processes?
- What can our organisation bring to a collaboration on these wider processes?

4 How does the corporate partner shape the market through processes of regulating?

- Which of these processes are affected by the partnership?
- What are the commercial reasons for the company to begin working together on those processes?
- What can our organisation bring to a collaboration on these wider processes?

5 What are our knowledge gaps in answering these questions, and how might we develop more insight on these processes?

In addition, if you have time and are working through this guidebook as a team, you could perform a role-play based on **Box 19**, applying it to a second- to third-generation transition conversation, rather than first- to second-generation.

After you have completed the previous exercises, you will likely have identified a range of information gaps, which you will need to work on, through both research and further conversations with your colleagues and corporate partners. Nevertheless, after the thinking that you have done, it is important at this stage to attempt to conceptualise a third-generation partnership, as this then helps you to see how the insights might be applied. The exercise in **Box 22** provides one way of doing that with **Exercise K**, which walks you through defining a transformation objective for a third-generation partnership. It adapts a 'soft systems' strategy planning methodology.

Box 22 **Clarifying a desired transformation and transformational partnership (Exercise K)**

Clarity on what system we are seeking to transform and the form of transformation we desire is key. A lasting and sizeable change in a social system requires prolonged and growing interactions from a part of that system. That 'part' is itself a system. Therefore what we can seek to do is create systems that will work toward the desired transformation in the system it sits within. A useful technique for being systematic in planning our systemic action has been developed by soft systems methodologists.[a] It involves being clear about the following aspects of any system we will create to transform larger systems:

- **Transformation**. The purpose of the system – what inputs are changed into what outputs?
- **Objects**. The people who will be acted upon (perhaps then becoming agents), either as 'immediate' and 'ultimate' beneficiaries of the proposed transformation, or even as 'victims'
- **Agents**. Those who should make the transformation happen – the people involved in making the system work
- **Worldview**. The perspective (including values) from which the transformation looks meaningful, desirable and possible
- **Environmental constraints**. Those factors that are taken as given in designing a system, such as the trends, events and demands of the political, legal, economic, social, demographic, technological, ethical, competitive and natural environments →

---

a P. Checkland and S. Howell, *Information, Systems and Information Systems: Making Sense of the Field* (Chichester, UK: Wiley, 1998). Note that the model presented here is a slight adaptation of their CATWOE in order to emphasise that the people affected are not necessarily 'clients' but beneficiaries, clients or even victims.

- **Owners**. Those who have the power to stop the transformation happening by stopping the system from working. (Note that owners, agents and targets can overlap)

This TOAWEO can help us come up with a root definition of the aim of a transformative alliance:

> The aim of the partnership is to become a system that transforms ____ [transformation] _____ by influencing ____ [objects]_____, as a result of the actions of ___ [agents] _____, enabled and justified by ___ [world-view] _____, with attention to wider ____ [environments] _____, and with the continuing support of ___ [owners] _____.

The root definition can define the transformation in broad and complex terms, or in more specific terms concerning the constituent parts. For instance, using a fictitious 'AIDS Awareness Alliance':

> The aim of the AIDS Awareness Alliance is to create a system that transforms the marketing services industry so it champions AIDS awareness within companies and to customers, by influencing the behaviours of marketing professionals, as a result of the actions of progressive people in marketing, design and media, enabled and justified by the growing recognition of their influence on AIDS challenges and solutions, with attention to wider trends in the marketing profession and with the continuing support of CARE International and a critical mass of marketing professionals.

Alternatively the 'transformation' in the root definition of this alliance could be more inwardly focused on the process of creation sought by bringing together people and resources within the partnership:

> The aim of the AIDS Awareness Alliance is to create a system that transforms the disparate elements of an NGO brand, resources, knowledge, and branding-related professionals interested in AIDS, into an effective movement to champion AIDS awareness within companies and to customers, by influencing the behaviours of all marketing professionals, as a result of the actions of progressive people in marketing, design and media, enabled and justified by the growing recognition of their influence on critical AIDS challenges and opportunities, with attention to wider trends in AIDS, and with the continuing support of CARE and a critical mass of marketing professionals.

Either use of the tool can help planning, although the more inward approach to defining the transformation means the latter definition of agents may not be necessary. This process is offered to help you use this approach in planning your own transformative partnership. →

Brainstorm on the various elements of a transformative partnership that relate to an existing partnership. Jot down and discuss initial ideas on the following:

Transformation. What is the broader system you would want to transform? What is the purpose of the system you want to create in order to do that – what inputs are changed into what outputs?

_____

_____

_____

Objects. Who are the people who will be acted upon, either as 'immediate' and 'ultimate' beneficiaries of the proposed transformation, or even as 'victims'?

_____

_____

_____

Agents. Who should make the transformation happen – the people involved in making the alliance work?

_____

_____

_____

Worldview. What perspective, including your values, makes this transformation seem meaningful, desirable and possible?

_____

_____

_____

Environmental constraints. What are the factors that you are taking as given in designing a system, such as the trends, events and demands of the political, legal, economic, social, demographic, technological, ethical, competitive and natural environments?

_____

_____

_____

Owners. Who has the power to stop the transformation happening by stopping the system from working? (There could be more than one.)

_____

_____

_____ →

Now develop a root definition for your potential transformative partnership.

The aim of the partnership is become a system
that transforms . . .   [transformation]

_____

by influencing . . .   [objects]

_____

as a result of the actions of . . .   [agents]

_____

enabled and justified by . . .   [world-view]

_____

with attention to wider . . .   [environments]

_____

and with the continuing support of . . .   [owners]

_____

You can re-jig the order and the phrases if you want. Finalise it below:

_____

_____

_____

_____

_____

_____

Note that you could also repeat this by preparing a root definition for a subsystem that would work on the larger system.

Reflections

- How different is the root definition from what you are currently working on through the partnership?
- What 'system' or (systems) do you need to create or engage with in order to encourage the creation of an actual transformative partnership?

Try the root definition process again for this system you need to create in your organisation or partnership to enable the generation of new ideas and commitment like the one you have just defined above.

The partnership concepts that you have developed as a result of these exercises may seem somewhat ambitious and difficult to win support for, both within your organisation and with existing business partners. To achieve wider support, it is useful to present examples of systemic partnerships, and also to engage colleagues in processes such as those outlined in this guidebook. The exercises presented in the guidebook were trialled in a workshop with the top aid agency CARE International UK. In the following year the participants in the workshop had played important roles in partnerships with industry that sought new levels of change in business practice in line with CARE International's mandate, such as the Ethical Tea Partnership mentioned earlier in this chapter and the work with Allianz (**Box 10**).

6 The challenges facing third-generation partners

The third generation of partnerships is relatively new, but already some benefits and limits can be identified (see **Box 23**).[1] The management of these partnerships is not a key topic in this guidebook, which is focused on the process of strategic review and planning, but it is important to at least highlight some emerging challenges, which will require conscious management. Such challenges are likely to centre around accountability issues, ranging from the difficulty of connecting systemic work to measurable, on-the-ground impacts, to questions about the legitimacy of new coalitions to influence governance or directly govern certain industries.

There are three key areas of risk for public-interest organisation participants in third-generation partnerships, in terms of how well they will deliver social change, that require conscious management.

---

1 Note that there is a difference between reasons for and against public-interest organisations attempting system change and attempting to work with companies on it. The table relates to the latter, i.e. the benefits and limits of partnering for systemic change rather than the benefits and limits of working towards such change.

The first challenge is to avoiding 'corporatism' by promoting transparency, accountability and the power of the less powerful stakeholders in the issues being addressed. 'Corporatism' is where elites and elite interests shape public policy to the exclusion of the general public. One important step in avoiding corporatist forms of partnership is to develop solid positions on matters of public policy and to have courage in sticking to those stances. The recent history of cross-sectoral climate policy collaboration suggests that many public-interest organisations have not developed and then adhered to an effective and fair policy position, rather seeking to have some involvement in a wrong-headed approach to the issue (see **Box 24**). As third-generation partnerships seek to influence power and often governance, their accountability to intended beneficiaries is even more important, in order to avoid corporatist effects. If partnership managers do not recognise the differences in resources of participants from different sectors of society, then relying on voluntary action from participants will lead to a privileging of powerful interests in the practical agenda of the partnership. Partnerships such as the UNGC and Finance Lab often rely on voluntary action from participants to create their work programmes. This is a response to limited funding and is regarded by some as a flexible and participative way of working. However, in practice it means that people from those institutions that have something to gain can stay engaged in the process, or people who have sufficient personal surplus through their prior choices in life (and exhibit characteristics related to that) can stay engaged. Whereas such voluntary contributions to these processes can and should be welcomed and encouraged, they needs to be complemented, and indeed (although not a term partnership practitioners like to hear) counteracted, by providing support for less well-resourced stakeholders to engage. Otherwise the rhetoric of participation can turn into something quite different. The case of the UNGC ten anniversary illustrates this problem rather well.

For the tenth anniversary, the consulting firm Accenture was invited to prepare a report on CEO opinions on corporate responsibility and sustainability – a report which set the tone for discussions at the Leaders Summit. On the one hand, it had some useful analysis of cross-cutting changes that are needed to mainstream corporate responsibility, such as changes to the investment practices and regulations to internalise more externalities.[2] It was promising for such ideas to be expressed by CEOs, as hitherto they

---

2   newsroom.accenture.com/article_display.cfm?article_id=5018

had only been discussed by more critical analysts.[3] On the other hand, the report and the research behind it appeared designed to make the participating businesses feel comfortable, avoiding challenging questions. The 766 CEOs who responded appeared very comfortable, with 81% agreeing that CR issues are 'fully embedded into the strategy and operations of my company'. Over 5,000 CEO members of the UNGC did not even respond to the opinion survey requested of them by the UN, but this was not discussed in the report. Delegate Dr Ven Pillay of the University of Pretoria wondered why CEOs were not asked direct questions such as whether they would have their bonuses linked to independent measures of their firm's social and environmental performance: surely not a worry for them if corporate responsibility is embedded in strategy and operations already?

Yes, the report was what one would expect from a consultancy that seeks to tickle, not ruffle, the feathers of c-suite executives. That 81% figure may do wonders in drumming up new business from CEOs who feel they are behind the game. In the past decade the UNGC has utilised the pro bono support of management consultants to establish its work programmes, and has been keen to appear a trusted and careful partner of business. Yet this reliance on pro bono input privileges certain views over others. The established consulting firms rarely challenge large corporations as they seek to serve them, and they rarely innovate ideas with impact because their business model does not allow time for a depth of reflection and research. After ten years the UNGC need not concern itself with appearing corporate-friendly and focus more on setting an ambitious change agenda, generating and disseminating methodologically sound, incisive and informative data on the realities of corporate responses to sustainable development. Otherwise, it risks becoming a corporatist organisation, putting out the views and policy positions of elite corporate interests.

For international development partnerships, this avoidance of corporatism is important, and makes it important to understand 'the needs of local partners and beneficiaries, with a focus on building their own capacity and capability rather than creating dependence', as was noted by the World Economic Forum.[4]

The second challenge is to avoid regarding the existence of a partnership and a partnership way of working as good in itself, regardless of

---

3   For instance, in the Lifeworth Annual Reviews (particularly *Serving Systemic Transformations*, 2005, and *Tipping Frames*, 2006), available from www.lifeworth. com/consult.

4   WEF, *Partnering for Success: Business Perspectives on Multistakeholder Partnerships* (Geneva: WEF, 2005): 11.

impacts relative to other potential strategies and tactics. This approach I term 'partnerism' and can lead to public-interest organisations divesting in the original drivers of business engagement, which include their critical thinking and campaigning on business issues. Critical analysis and exhortation have been key to creating contexts for third-generation partnerships to emerge, and this pressure will need maintaining even when working at deeper levels of collaboration. To avoid 'partnerism', the various tools, approaches and moods of partnership working need to be seen in context. If participative dialogues shapes what is considered or voiced as valid or important knowledge, then that can be positive in some cases: for instance, if it helps communicate the views of women workers in sweatshops or paddy fields. Therefore, in development work, participative approaches to policy making have been an important tool in combating technocratic approaches that override local interests, views and values. However, such participative, non-technical approaches can be unhelpful in other contexts. In gatherings of diverse professions in middle-class or elite settings that are focused on social or environmental problems, to use participative processes to identify their concerns and sense of agency, is not so useful. That is because those professionals have not suffered from a systematic overriding of their lived experiences by technocratic experts, while the issues they are discussing are usually more systemic and complex than, say, the conditions in one's village or factory.

An aspect of the emerging ideology of partnerism is to value convivial participative processes in and of themselves, rather than as a tool of potential but debatable use. An emphasis on convivial participative process can then lead to replication and justification of existing power relations and discourses, quite the opposite of the argument that it generates innovation and breakthrough. Some angst, anger and argument can be as authentic and insightful as placid acquiescence to a facilitator's interest in creating a nice experience for participants in a group process. What is most important is the goal, not the process. It is the best illustration of the new ideology of partnerism that some facilitators and conveners of partnerships see the process as at least important as the goal, and even *as* the goal.

Managing the dangers of corporatism and partnerism relates to a third key challenge for third-generation partnership conveners – developing expertise in responsible social transformation. As the goal of third-generation partnerships concern transformation, greater clarity on what the needed transformations are, how to pursue them and how to evaluate one's efforts will be key. It is important to move beyond rhetoric about bold partnerships and develop ways of measuring the partnership's impact and outcome that relate to real change. For instance, results reported by the ninemillion.org campaign in 2010 for delivered projects were rather modest in comparison to the brand profile, and no data on lifestyle changes were available.[5] Outcomes such as impacts on public opinion can be measured and should be if they are claimed as part of the aim of a partnership.

In designing one's activities to promote social change, it is important to draw on insights from diverse social and political sciences. The phrase 'tipping point' was used throughout the UNGC Leaders Summit. As I mentioned at the start of the book, this was important in reflecting a new ambition from within the UNGC to promote more systemic change. However, as any social scientist who has read Malcolm Gladwell's book of that title will understand, there is no clear theory of what a 'tipping point' is or how it is reached. If our topic here is how to create systemic change, where sufficient numbers of individuals or organisations change in order to re-pattern the way most of us behave, then there are many of fields of social science that we can draw on. Draw on them we must, if we are to be serious and not rhetorical about seeking systemic change through our cross-sector partnering.

Insights on social change processes (in society and in meetings) can come from organisational change management, marketing, innovation and entrepreneurship, behavioural economics, social movements studies, network sciences, systems theories and cybernetics, institutional theory, social psychology, sociologies of power, design thinking, theories of art practice, and more. We need to find ways to draw on such fields, integrate their insights and make them practical for practitioners and policy makers.

Two examples of the application of schools of thought on social change to the corporate responsibility field are social movements theory[6] and network sciences.[7] However, the fields receiving the most attention are those that are most known to management consultants – such as marketing (the basis of most of the evidence in *Tipping Point*), and organisational change management (for instance, the current popularity of the U-process to structure the design and facilitation of change-oriented meetings). It is not certain that the leading management consultants recognise the wealth of knowledge

5   NineMillion.org, 'Results' (2010); www.ninemillion.org/index.php?/site/Sections/Results (accessed 26 August 2010).

6   Jem Bendell (ed.), *The Corporate Responsibility Movement: Five Years of Global Corporate Responsibility Analysis from Lifeworth, 2001–2005* (Sheffield, UK: Greenleaf Publishing, 2009; www.greenleaf-publishing.com/crmovement).

7   Jem Bendell and Annekathrin Ellersiek, *Noble Networks? Advocacy for Global Justice and the 'Network Effect'* (Geneva: UNRISD, 2009).

on social change. For instance, the elite consulting firm McKinsey published a matrix on social change, suggesting it as a new contribution,[8] when it was an unintentional recycling of philosopher Ken Wilber's four-quadrant model of the locations of change.[9]

If the Leaders Summit marks the beginning of a wider acknowledgement among the corporate responsibility and sustainable business professions of the need to serve systemic transformations, it needs to be followed rapidly by a new awareness about where to learn about such change. The famous management consultancies may not be the places to look for the relevant expertise, as there is a level of conceptual development required that costs time and money that most consulting firms can not afford.

Not only is becoming smarter about social change processes a key imperative for people engaged in cross-sector partnering, but so is the need to be smarter about the ethics of shaping such change. For instance, the UNGC is said by some to be part of an emerging global governance architecture.[10] If initiatives like the UNGC and other private regulatory initiatives do achieve such power that governance is a useful term to describe their role, then this raises further issues of accountability and fairness. In whose name do they govern?[11] A prerequisite for addressing this issue and developing appropriate processes is for it to be recognised as warranting attention. Too often when people raise these issues, including at the Leaders Summit, senior business people cite how their businesslike approach means they do not have time for such philosophical debates. Their partners in public-interest organisations must not take that as an acceptable answer. Responsible social transformation will require a deeper reflection on the ethics of the work we do.

In preparing this guidebook I have sought to distil some lessons from some areas of social and political science and turn them into exercises for your strategic review and planning of cross-sector partnering. It is just a start: there remains much more work to do to transpose the huge fields of academic knowledge into tools for reflective practitioners.

---

8   John Elkington, 'A New Paradigm for Change', *What Matters*, 6 April 2010; what-matters.mckinseydigital.com/social_entrepreneurs/a-new-paradigm-for-change.

9   Ken Wilber, *A Theory of Everything: An Integral Vision for Business, Politics, Science and Spirituality* (Shambhala Publications, 2000). (Note that it is not an actual model of change, but a tool for helping people to think outside and inside their existing focus for the object of their change intention.)

10   craneandmatten.blogspot.com/2010/06/elephant-in-room.html

11   For a discussion of this issue see J. Bendell, 'In Whose Name? The Accountability of Corporate Social Responsibility', *Development in Practice* 15.3–4 (June 2005): 362–74.

With third-generation partnerships the stakes are raised, as the ambitions and potential impacts are far greater. Consequently the character of the individuals involved in them will be key. As with any area of professional life, there will be internal conflicts between staff due to people placing different importance on different things. Many people will succumb to partnerism, and lose sight of the goal. It will require courage from others to challenge them and to ensure that principles of effectiveness, efficiency, fairness and accountability are upheld.

At the beginning of this guidebook I mentioned my work with WWF-UK in the mid 1990s. What I did not mention is that I got sacked from WWF-UK. Looking back, I believe I was let go because I would not succumb to partnerism. I was always thinking about how our impact on forest conservation could be maximised, as that was why I had joined the organisation. I was also always considering whether the NGO was being compromised. I saw that the size of the group of companies that were working to buy wood from sustainable sources was limited by the resources of WWF-UK; the team on this project usually consisted of myself and an older, part-time consultant, who managed the membership of 40-plus companies. I did not think it would be right for the companies to pay fees to WWF-UK to cover the costs of their membership, as this would compromise the independence of WWF-UK. However, I did not think the group should not grow. I thought we should go to a thousand companies – why not? Therefore I suggested to my colleagues that we accredit an independent consultancy to run the group, and manage the companies' membership responsibilities, and that WWF-UK would inspect the operations of that consultancy to ensure the company members were meeting the required standards. The consultancy could charge a fee per member company.

This was one of a number of ideas that I was putting forward, way beyond my station as a lowly staff member doing data support and analysis. Because I did not have a personal agenda I was confident in my views being good for the organisation. However, this did not go down well with the older consultant – perhaps he did not want the scope of our work to change – and he said to our boss that he could not work with me any more. The boss, an ambitious guy, always travelling, much younger than the consultant, had bigger things to focus on, and did not become involved in sorting out the problem, so fixed it by letting me go. Maybe that was the best decision for him and the project was given other priorities. At the time it energised me even further, and I set up a consultancy and wrote the book and various articles that then helped the wider movement of corporate responsibility. I also continued to work with many WWF staff as a consultant on some exciting partnerships, so do not perceive a particular problem with this important organisation. However, I tell this personal story here as a warning that partnerships create their own dynamics, their own self-interests, and that it takes courage to push for greater social change.

Clarifying the role of multi-stakeholder initiatives in global governance

Different types of public-interest organisation face different issues in their private-sector engagement. As UN agencies play a role in international law and provide technical advice on national regulation, they face particular challenges in how they manage their engagement with business. The concept of multi-stakeholder participation in addressing public issues has become popular in the international policy sphere in the last ten years. This thinking has led UN agencies encouraging the adoption of multi-stakeholder approaches by its member states. The Food and Agriculture Organization (FAO) advises that:

> States are encouraged to apply a multi-stakeholder approach to national food security to identify the roles of and involve all relevant stakeholders, encompassing civil society and private sector, drawing together their know-how with a view to facilitate the efficient use of resources.

The embrace of multi-stakeholder initiatives (MSIs), and with it more corporate engagement, has not come without complication. In 2004 a BBC television programme revealed how a key consultation into how much sugar we should be eating was secretly funded by the sugar industry. The BBC uncovered documents which reveal the World Sugar Research Organisation and International Life Sciences Institute (ILSI), both funded by the sugar industry, helped pay for the Expert Consultation on Carbohydrates in Human Nutrition, which made recommendations to the World Health Organization (WHO) and in turn other bodies and governments. The BBC revealed that ILSI was given the opportunity to suggest members of the committee and to select the chairman, as well as to review the agenda of the consultation. 'I believe that it would be impossible to produce an unbiased report when the source of funding came from groups with clearly vested interests,' explained Professor Jim Mann, a committee member. The experts the BBC spoke to claimed that they had agreed a limit of between 55% and 75% for how much carbohydrate we should eat, but when the report came out the upper limit had gone. Professor Mann explained:

> It would clearly be to the advantage of the industry not to have an upper limit, because increasingly the industry are producing food products which are reduced in fat, and one way of compensating for fat is to increase the amount of sugar . . . So obviously if there's no upper limit of sugar, one can add sugar with impunity into a whole range of food products.[12]

The influence of pharmaceutical companies at the WHO has been a cause for concern for some years. One particular case highlights a conflict between commercial and public interest, and how UN agencies can become agents for commercial interests if they do not take precautions. Treatment guidelines endorsed by the WHO have worldwide impact, influencing national policies and the guidelines given to doctors. The WHO receives more private money than it gets in dues from member nations. Daphne Fresle, a former official in the WHO, resigned in protest, complaining of the UN agency's relationships with drug makers, because 'WHO higher-ups routinely censored internal disagreements among staff members over drug-company influence on the agency.'[13]

In 1998, the WHO set out to advise doctors around the world on how to treat high blood pressure. For years, doctors had considered 120/80 mmHg to be the ideal blood pressure and anything under 140 mmHg to be healthy.

The agency turned for advice to experts at the World Heart Federation. They named Dr Alberto Zanchetti, an Italian cardiologist, to head a committee to examine and update the guidelines for hypertension. Zanchetti appointed the other 17 members of the committee; all but one 'had close financial ties to drug firms', according to the *Seattle Times*. They reported that Zanchetti was paid to consult and give speeches for Recordati, Italy's largest drug company, which sells a blood pressure drug available in 43 countries and awaiting approval in the United States. The paper also stated that Zanchetti took grants or consulting fees from 18 other drug companies; however, the WHO did not require him to disclose how much money the industry pays him. 'Zanchetti insisted on lower blood-pressure targets and

12   BBC, 'UN Probes Sugar Industry Claims', 8 October 2004; news.bbc.co.uk/2/hi/ health/3726510.stm.
13   D. Wilson, 'New Blood-Pressure Guidelines Pay Off – For Drug Companies', *Seattle Times*, 26 June 2005; seattletimes.nwsource.com/html/health/sick1.html.

made sweeping statements endorsing the safety of newer drugs', reported the *Seattle Times*. Dr Arne Melander, a Malmö University professor and chief of Sweden's government Network of Drug Epidemiology, was:

> ... disturbed when I started looking into this, that so few people could influence so much, and that these megaphones for the pharmaceutical industry had become more powerful ... Study after study was carried out by Dr Hansson, Zanchetti and the group, hoping for something that would finally give evidence that the newer drugs were better.

The resulting 1999 WHO hypertension guideline recommended that doctors, as a first course of treatment, pick from any of the five classes of hypertension drugs, rather than the cheaper and safety-proven use of diuretics and beta-blockers. Zanchetti and company proposed a much lower threshold for healthy blood pressure. As a result, suddenly, nearly half the world's population was now classified as hypertensive or 'prehypertensive' (a newly invented condition), including three-quarters of the elderly population.[14]

The new guideline was an ideal marketing tool for drug companies, who began communicating the findings to doctors around the world. A protest against the findings was signed by 888 doctors, pharmacists and scientists from 58 countries. Their petition said the committee had misrepresented medical evidence and the WHO had 'failed its responsibility' to improve care and prevent unnecessary deaths. A few years later, the largest hypertension study ever – funded solely by the US federal government – concluded that the newer blood pressure drugs are less safe, usually no more effective and far more expensive than decades-old drugs such as diuretics. Despite the evidence, market share for the older drugs continues to drop, with sales of diuretics and beta-blockers falling 35% and 52%, respectively, between 1998 and 2007.[15]

This danger of unhelpful business influence on standard setting was in our minds when advising the UN Standing Committee on Nutrition (UNSCN) on the development of a private-sector engagement strategy and policy. We therefore sought to find ways to facilitate engagement on specific projects, while ensuring that the UNSCN remained independent and its technical and policy advisory roles would not be influenced by companies, other than through the normal requests for information by its committees.

Particular issues arise for MSIs that become involved in setting standards or providing technical advice that can influence national regulations and

14   *Ibid.*
15   *Ibid.*

international law. Many third-generation partnerships are emerging in the field of lobbying and advocacy, as well as private standard setting, and therefore these issues will become more pertinent in future years. There is an urgent need for greater clarity about appropriate business engagement in multi-stakeholder initiatives that affect regulations and public policy. That clarity must start from understanding the arguments for why it is beneficial for non-state actors, such as business and NGOs, to engage in global policy processes (including dialogues and specific projects) – rationales that are often misunderstood by proponents and critics of MSIs.

The first reason relates to democratisation, and to NGOs with grassroots connections. Intergovernmental processes do not represent all persons affected by decisions made about regulations and interventions. This is because many governments are not democratic, and if they are electoral democracies, some do not have a mandate from the majority of their populations and, even if they do, the minorities are not always well represented (certain ethnic groups or social classes may be excluded from representation in government, for example). Therefore, by having a voice in global policy processes, those organisations with connections to such citizens can add to the democratic credentials of these processes, and thus their legitimacy (if democracy is understood as a situation where persons affected by decisions have an equal ability to influence those decisions). This is an argument for some NGOs to have a voice in certain policy debates, but not a vote. It is also an argument against, not for, large corporations to be involved in these processes, as they already have significant influence over national politics and legally they represent private owners and have responsibility towards shareholders, which are a small and privileged portion of the people affected by public policies. However, the other key rationales for non-state actor involvement also apply to companies.

The second rationale for non-state actor involvement is that the technical quality, rather than democratic quality, of dialogues and activities is improved by involving people with different and additional resources, knowledge, skills, experiences, values and assumptions. This is one argument for companies to be engaged in dialogues as well as NGOs. However, to balance this technical aspect with the political issue described above requires regulating the nature of corporate participation in policy dialogues, and their influence over the outcomes of those dialogues, as well as other activities.

The third rationale relates not to the quality of the initiatives and deliberations in democratic or technical terms, but to the impact on the participants themselves. Participation in a public policy dialogue or a joint project may have a democratising impact on the participants. To understand the concerns of others and focus on the collective interest during a deliberation or joint project may enhance the awareness and democratic commitment of individual participants. This suggests that all non-state actors, including companies, can be engaged to help change them and thus benefit those who interact with them beyond the specific initiative. However, this is a contested hypothesis, and so steps should be taken to promote commitment and learning from corporations, in relation to expressed intention of an initiative, and to evaluate the level of commitment and action arising from corporate partners as a result of their participation.

A fourth rationale for non-state actor participation in intergovernmental dialogues and initiatives is that the outcomes, such as standards and policies, often concern non-state actors, so their participation might increase their ownership of outcomes, and thus enhance their commitment to their implementation.

Many MSI managers and proponents do not articulate these rationales clearly, with multi-stakeholder processes often simply assumed to be desirable. The rationales I have just outlined imply that MSIs must be managed in order to capture the benefits while reducing the risks associated with them.

MSIs are not without criticisms, however. Some argue that the alleged benefits of MSIs are still mostly unproven, and they can, instead, be counterproductive. As described earlier, a key concern is that they facilitate corporate lobbying and thus can lead to regulatory capture of governmental and intergovernmental institutions, so they do not serve the public interest as they might. Others question the accountability of MSIs to their supposed beneficiaries, and whether the issues and actions they identify are the most relevant and appropriate. Others argue that the outcomes of MSIs, such as codes and standards, are often not well implemented.[16]

Despite these concerns, some NGOs and intergovernmental bodies have embraced MSIs without first clarifying their political and ethical basis and defining their vision for the private sector, and their strategy for attaining that vision. The particular challenges faced by UN agencies have not been well understood by many partnership advisers, educators and brokers, and therefore some risky partnering practices have emerged across the UN system. It is an essential first step for any intergovernmental agency to define

---

16 See Jem Bendell, *Barricades and Boardrooms: A Contemporary History of the Corporate Accountability Movement* (Geneva: UNRISD, 2004): 13.

its vision of the private sector's relationship to the agency's goals, and then adapt procedures to be able to engage corporations while upholding the independence and integrity of their work. Unfortunately, in the majority of cases in the UN system, this approach has not being taken, and therefore risks of unhelpful corporate influence exist. From my perspective, this arises from a lack of leadership within the UN system, with companies too often regarded as either an unproblematic donor or an irrelevance.

Box 23 **Some illustrative benefits and limits of third-generation partnerships**

Group	Benefits	Limits
Public-interest organisations	Leveraging corporate influence	Low member or media interest
	Accessing technical expertise	Stretching traditional expertise and mandates
Business	Influencing regulation	Time-consuming
	Influencing consumers	Uncomfortable transparency
Government	Greater support for intervention	New diverse political coalitions
	Smarter civil servants	More complex intergovernmental processes
Intended beneficiaries	New avenues of influence	Variable accountabilities
	Ambitious agendas	Protracted processes
Wider society	Innovation on public issues	Undermining electoral process
	Participation opportunities	Corporate influence in politics

Refer to **Box 4** for explanation of the groups.

Box 24 **Problems with partnerships for carbon cap-and-trade**

Groups such as the Climate Disclosure Project and the Institutional Investors Group on Climate Change, and the Business Leaders Initiative on Climate Change, now bring together large swathes of the private-sector that lobby privately and advocate publicly on the need for an intergovernmental agreement on climate change. One the one hand, this is very promising, representing a wiser approach to business that recognises systemic threats to value creation and the role of government to provide frameworks for innovation.

On the other hand, this corporate involvement in public policy development presents a threat to effective action on curbing climate change. To understand that, we must understand the history, limitations and injustices of cap-and-trade systems.

→

The focus of discussions of the UN Framework Convention on Climate Change (UNFCCC) has been about capping carbon emissions and mechanisms to trade permits to pollute the atmosphere with carbon. The Kyoto Protocol established the concept of carbon offsets, where an enterprise can be financed to adopt technologies or practices to reduce its current or predicted carbon emissions and the reduction in emissions can be deducted from the company or government paying for the necessary changes. The UN Clean Development Mechanism (CDM) resulted from this approach, as did the development of carbon emissions trading schemes (ETS). The reason that this was adopted as the best policy option in 1997, when the protocol was adopted, was that the United States, and then Vice-President Al Gore, proposed it as the only option it would sign. This was after intensive lobbying by Enron, the corrupt company, that had profited a lot from trading in energy derivatives and the cap-and-trade sulphur market in the US.

The reason for the focus on cap-and-trade, and the reason for it being adopted by other governments since, is simple – of all the policy tools available, it posed the least threat to the polluting industries, and offered the creation of a whole new market for financial service providers. Other options, such as outlawing certain practices or introducing carbon taxes, were therefore sidelined at that time in intergovernmental negotiations. For instance, a carbon tax was proposed at the EU level during the 1990s but failed due to industrial lobbying.[a]

A focus on cap-and-trade at the UNFCCC negotiations has been a waste because carbon cap-and-trade systems are ineffective, inefficient, unfair, unworkable and extremely difficult to agree at an intergovernmental level and can alienate people from decisive action on carbon emissions.[b]

Cap-and-trade is **ineffective** in delivering real cuts in carbon emissions, according to the top climate scientists and economists who have invented it. One example of its ineffectiveness comes from the post-Soviet states. The Soviet Union was given a huge allocation of carbon emissions permits in the early 1990s. Johann Hari in *The Independent* explained it like this:

> The following year, [the Soviet Union] collapsed, and its industrial base went into freefall – along with its carbon emissions. It was

a David Pearce, *The United Kingdom Climate Change Levy: A Study in Political Economy* (OECD Environment Directorate, Centre for Tax Policy and Administration, 2005; www.olis.oecd.org/olis/2004doc.nsf/LinkTo/NT00009492/$FILE/JT00179396.pdf, accessed 30 August 2009).

b Larry Lohmann (ed.), *Carbon Trading: A Critical Conversation on Climate Change, Privatisation and Power* (Dag Hammarskjold Foundation, Durban Group for Climate Justice and The Corner House, UK, 2006; www.thecornerhouse.org.uk/summary.shtml?x=544225).

never going to release those gases after all. But Russia and the Eastern European countries have held on to them in all negotiations as 'theirs'. Now, they are selling them to rich countries who want to purchase 'cuts'. Under the current system, the US can buy them from Romania and say they have cut emissions – even though they are nothing but a legal fiction.

Those permits account for 10 gigatonnes of CO_2, which dwarf the 6 gigatonne savings that would come from the entire developed world cutting its emissions by 40% by 2020. Another aspect of ineffectiveness is how cuts through carbon trading are recorded twice. Hari explains:

> If Britain pays China to abandon a coal power station and construct a hydro-electric dam instead, Britain pockets the reduction in carbon emissions . . . [so it can] keep a coal power station open at home. But at the same time, China also counts this change as part of its overall cuts. So one tonne of carbon cuts is counted twice. This means the whole system is riddled with exaggeration – and the figure for overall global cuts is a con.[c]

Cap-and-trade systems are **inefficient and unfair**. Permits for polluting are allocated to current large polluters, who then make a disproportionate profit from carbon trading. Patrick O'Connor and Alex Safari explain it thus:

> In the lead-up to the handout of carbon credits in Europe, the major polluters lobbied their national governments and ratcheted up reported emissions in order to claim many more credits than they actually required. Once the market came into effect in January 2005 they then returned to business as usual. Without reducing any emissions, businesses were able to sell their surplus credits for significant sums. British oil companies BP and Shell, for example, made £17.9 million and £20.7 million ($40 million and $46 million) respectively through the sale of their carbon credits.[d]

The carbon trades are conducted by financial institutions, who charge fees that accrue to shareholders, not to those needing to adapt to climate changes or rising prices. These financial institutions also create derivatives, which lead to speculative activities that benefit only themselves, and impose an unnecessary cost on economic systems →

c Johann Hari, 'Leaders of the Rich World are Enacting a Giant Fraud: Corporate Lobbyists can Pressure or Bribe Governments to Rig the System in their Favour', *The Independent*, 11 December 2009; www.independent.co.uk/opinion/commentators/ johann-hari/johann-hari-leaders-of-the-rich-world-are-enacting-a-giant-fraud-1837963.html.

d Patrick O'Connor and Alex Safari, 'Climate Change, Kyoto, and Carbon Trading', 7 November 2007; www.sep.org.au/articles07/clim-071107.html.

and consumers. Today the carbon trading market is worth over $100 billion.[e] The problem with this behaviour is its effect on society and on attempts to curb carbon emissions in socially acceptable ways.

Cap-and-trade systems are also currently **unworkable**, with huge levels of fraud. Fox News reported that 'the top cops in Europe say carbon-trading has fallen prey to an organized crime scheme that has robbed the continent of $7.4 billion'.[f] Globally applied cap-and-trade systems are also **internationally improbable**, as national allocations of carbon caps are extremely difficult to agree at an intergovernmental level. The co-editor of *The Economics and Politics of Climate Change*, Cameron Hepburn, points out that seeking agreement on caps and allocations puts difficult issues of distribution and compensation at the heart of international negotiations, which has clearly contributed to the impasse.[g] The past 18 years of climate negotiations have shown how difficult it is for governments to agree on caps and allocations.

The fifth main way that a cap-and-trade focus is hindering global action on climate change is that it is **alienating** some of the public from action on carbon emissions. Much of the media that is critical of any action on climate change focuses on the scam that is carbon cap-and-trade. Rather than arguing for effective, efficient and fair action on climate change, the majority of the anti cap-and-trade analysis rejects action on climate change altogether.

Given all these limitations it should be no surprise that some government leaders were critical of the West's approach. The President of Bolivia exclaimed: 'Capitalism wants to address climate change with carbon markets. We denounce those markets and the countries which [promote them]. It's time to stop making money from the disgrace that they have perpetrated.'[h]

For there to begin to be total reductions in carbon emissions through behaviour change and technological innovations, 'you have to put an honest price on carbon, which is going to have to gradually rise over time', explains climate scientist James Hansen.[i] As prices will rise, the mechanism for doing that will need to be broadly perceived as →

e   Oscar Reyes, 'Taking Care of Business', *The New Internationalist*, December 2009; www.newint.org/features/2009/12/01/corporate-influence.

f   Fox News, 'Fraud in Europe's Cap and Trade System a "Red Flag," Critics Say', 2009; politics.foxnews.mobi/quickPage.html?page=21292&content=28795207&pageNum=-1.

g   Tim Harford, 'Political Ill Wind Blows a Hole in the Climate Change Debate', *Financial Times*, 28 November 2009; timharford.com/2009/11/political-ill-wind-blows-a-hole-in-the-climate-change-debate.

h   Evo Morales, 'Bolivia Stuns Climate Summit with Target', *The Hindu*, 18 December 2009: 15; www.hindu.com/2009/12/18/stories/2009121855951500.htm.

i   James Hansen interviewed by Amy Goodman, *Democracy Now*, 22 December 2009; www.democracynow.org/2009/12/22/leading_climate_scientist_james_hansen_on.

socially legitimate. There is a great history of struggles against unfair taxes, such as the British salt taxes in India to the poll taxes imposed in the 1980s in the UK. If the polluters and bankers are receiving the cash from price rises and there is no immediate and corresponding reduction in carbon emissions, there will be a justified and overwhelming backlash. The social legitimacy of any system for increasing the price of carbon is therefore key, and should be the focus of intergovernmental deliberations.

We need to encourage behaviour change, guide innovations and invest in helping people maintain or develop their quality of life while limiting their carbon emissions and adapting to the increasing impacts of climate change. A globally agreed, nationally implemented, carbon tax, applied upstream at the point of energy production for commercial distribution, would have been far simpler to agree and implement than the cap-and-trade approach pursued since 1997. Arguments against such a global carbon charge include that it would fund unaccountable governance, or would be socially regressive, or could not specify limits for carbon emissions. Each argument is woefully mistaken, as I have detailed elsewhere.[j]

The intergovernmental paralysis that has been caused over the last 18 years by seeking agreements on carbon caps, the daylight robbery of both taxpayers and consumers that current carbon markets have aided, and their complete ineffectiveness in reducing real carbon emissions, means that a fresh paradigm is called for. It is becoming clear that the only responsible thing for companies and financial institutions to do is to call for a new global framework for carbon taxation, and an end to ineffective and unfair carbon cap-and-trade markets. Public-interest organisations need to develop their own understanding of climate policy and engage companies from that standpoint, being prepared to stand up to ineffective, inefficient and unfair policy proposals.

j   Jem Bendell, 'Climate Leadership' (Occasional Paper, Lifeworth Consulting, 2010; www.lifeworth.com/consult/2010/01/climateleadership).

7 The particular opportunities and challenges of third-generation partnerships for development

In recent years more business executives have expressed commitment to making a positive contribution to social development across the world. This is illustrated by new awards schemes to recognise business leadership in meeting the Millennium Development Goals (MDGs), such as the 'Inclusive Business Challenge'[1] and the World Business and Development Awards.[2] Mr Jean Rozwadowski, Secretary-General of the International Chamber of Commerce (ICC), has argued that 'increasingly the private sector is a critical component for increasing aid effectiveness and achieving the Millennium

---

1 World Business Council for Sustainable Development, 'WBCSD Launches "Inclusive Business Challenge"', 22 April 2010; www.wbcsd.org/Plugins/DocSearch/details.asp?DocTypeId=251&ObjectId=MzgyMjA.

2 Business Call to Action, '2010 World Business and Development Awards Launched', 20 May 2010; bcta-initiative.org/2010/05/20/2010-world-business-and-development-awards-launched-2.

Development Goals'.[3] Positive contributions of business to development have been highlighted by the work of the National Committee for International Cooperation and Sustainable Development (NCDO)[4] and the UNGC. In *The Global Compact for Development* the UN initiative presents a range of initiatives and support for business to contribute to development, and in *Innovating for a Brighter Future: The Role of Business in Achieving the MDGs* they discuss progress made since 2000 on this agenda through the work of the Global Compact. This growing attention to the role of business in development means that it is an important area to examine for potential cross-sector partnerships, and in particular, the types of partnerships that address the root causes of maldevelopment. In this chapter the issues arising for cross-sector development partnerships are explored, and some recommendations offered for what to look for in potential business partners.

Before progressing, let us take a moment to reflect on the history of business and development. It is important to note that business did development before development did development. By this statement I mean that business is the process of making and trading things with and for each other and is therefore a process through which people, families and societies advance – the very meaning of 'development'. It has only been since the late 1940s that the modern concept of international development as a project that would be pursued by national aid agencies, international bodies and non-governmental organisations began to take shape.[5] In the past few years this 'international development community', which I consider myself part of, has begun to engage business in new ways, rather than simply through seeking its regulation by government for more social development gain. In addition, with the rise in voluntary acceptance of corporate responsibility for impacts on society, and new creative thinking about how social and environmental challenges can become drivers of innovation, companies have been looking again at the preoccupations of the international development community. Much can be learned by business from international development experts, and vice versa.

One area of focus within the business community is how to do more business at the Bottom, or Base, of the economic Pyramid (BoP), meaning the

---

3   *Ibid.*

4   NCDO, 'Business Impact Report 2010: Scanning the Contribution of 20 Multinationals to the Millennium Development Goals'; ncdo.nl/docs/uploads/Business%20Impact%20Report%202010.pdf or click on Download het volledige rapport (Engelstalig) at ncdo.nl/Nieuws/Business_impact_report.

5   Jem Bendell, *Barricades and Boardrooms: A Contemporary History of the Corporate Accountability Movement* (Geneva: UNRISD, 2004).

billions of people who live on very limited means.[6] BoP discussions and initiatives centre on the development of products for the poor in ways that are commercially viable. The type of initiatives praised and the problems with these from a deeper development understanding highlight how there is still much to be learned. As Anand Kumar, assistant professor of marketing at IIMA, has pointed out, many existing BoP initiatives fail to target those who are truly needy. Instead, many corporations engaged in BoP focus on providing non-essential products to those with disposable income.[7] Some BoP initiatives also see large multinational corporations displacing local competition and local labour by importing goods, materials and labour.[8] Too often there is a net benefit for the multinational corporation but no enduring benefit to the disadvantaged communities in the form of employment or infrastructure.[9] As Aneel Karnani, associate professor of strategy at the University of Michigan, suggests, the eradication of deprivation will require firms to buy from the poor,[10] instead of simply selling to them.[11] Furthermore, Suparna Chatterjee, adjunct to the department of economics at Xavier University, suggests that:

> there is very little evidence that selling to the poor is a profitable venture which benefits large companies as well as the poor ... [and] one must not just talk about fortune at the bottom of the pyramid but also fortune for the bottom of the pyramid.[12]

The main fallacy of BoP approaches has been to assume that reducing prices through techniques such as smaller servings constitutes a form of social development, when if these are simply consumer goods then it does nothing about the problem of people being cash-poor. The implications

---

6   Stefan Stern, 'Manifesto Writer for Business Survival', *Financial Times Online*, 18 April 2010; www.ft.com/cms/s/0/35ed5a1a-4add-11df-a7ff-00144feab49a,dwp_uuid=02e16f4a-46f9-11da-b8e5-00000e2511c8.html.

7   Anand Kumar Jaiswal, 'The Fortune at the Bottom or the Middle of the Pyramid?', *MIT Press Journals* 3.1 (2008): 85.

8   Jem Bendell, 'From Responsibility to Opportunity: CSR and the Future of Corporate Contributions to World Development', *MHCi Monthly Feature*, February 2005.

9   Jem Bendell, 'Making Business Work for Development: Rethinking Corporate Social Responsibility', *id21 insights* 54.4 (2005): 1.

10   Andrew Crabtree, 'Evaluating the Bottom of the Pyramid from a Fundamental Capabilities Perspective', 2007; www.cbs.dk/content/view/pub/38201.

11   Aneel Karnani, 'The Mirage of Marketing to the Bottom of the Pyramid: How the Private Sector Can Help Alleviate Poverty', *California Management Review* 47.4 (2007): 90.

12   Suparna Chatterjee, 'Selling to the Poor: Reflection, Critique and Dialogue', 2009; warrington.ufl.edu/academics/pdbp/docs/proposals/2009_SuparnaChatterjee.pdf.

here for public-interest organisations working on development are three-fold. First is to recognise that some large companies are interested in finding new ways to provide products and services to the poor and therefore could present useful partners in meeting social needs in a self-financing way, which would help reach many people. Second is to recognise that, to do so, companies can benefit from the participation of NGOs and development agencies and that gives such organisations some leverage to influence what kind of products and services are provided and in what ways. Third is to seek to use this leverage by identifying the products and services that will support sustainable development, and forms of production and trade of those products or services that will support local economic empowerment, rather than outcompeting local alternatives. The CARE International partnership with Allianz for micro-insurance is a good example of a BoP partnership as it does not outcompete local alternatives and provides a service with broader positive development impacts (**Box 10**).

There are now numerous instances of enterprise being undertaken to deliver specific development impacts, which is often called 'social enterprise'.[13] The concept of social enterprise appears more useful than BoP as the examples discussed usually have a clear social purpose at their heart, rather than seeing the poor as simply a new market for making a fortune. Seeking enterprise solutions to social challenges of all kinds is an important approach, as it promises scale without reliance on continued charity. The success of the Grameen group of companies was discussed earlier. Its philosophy of solving social problems through new approaches to enterprise has found many new applications. For instance, a severe energy shortage in Bangladesh contributes to its environmental degradation, poverty and inequality.[14] Therefore the Grameen Bank sought to combat this by providing solar technology to individual households at the same cost as kerosene.[15] Since the project began in 1996, the Grameen Bank reports it has installed more than 285,000 solar hot water systems, constructed 7,000 biogas stoves, produced 40,000 improved cooking stoves, created 20,000 green jobs and trained 3,000 women as renewable energy technicians.[16] With such compelling stories of change, the community engaged in social enterprise is the

---

13 Social enterprise was first discussed in the 'World Review', *Journal of Corporate Citizenship* 13 (2003), and in eight subsequent reviews.

14 World Future Council, 'Bringing Green Energy, Health, Income and Green Jobs to rural Bangladesh', 2009; www.worldfuturecouncil.org/fileadmin/user_upload/Presentations/Grameen_Shakti_Bangladesh_Part_1.pdf.

15 *Ibid.*

16 *Ibid.*

most dynamic in the field of business–society relations, demonstrated by enthusiastic participation in the Skoll Foundation and Schwab Foundation forums on social entrepreneurship in recent years.[17]

The implications of social enterprise for larger corporations are not entirely clear at present. Jack Sim, of the World Toilet Organisation (WTO), which works with Unilever and Ikea, and develops social enterprises to promote sanitation worldwide, believes that 'social enterprise can act as a bridge educating companies about the need and opportunity to alleviate poverty'.[18] He is hopeful that more companies will cross that bridge. However, most social enterprises rarely involve international companies in ways that meet the companies' normal expected return on investment, and therefore large companies participate in a partly philanthropic fashion. This presents a key limitation to the ability to involve large corporations in ways that could achieve scale and thus wider systemic impact. However, the experience of Grameen demonstrates that there are opportunities for partnership with large corporations, as they have done with Telenor, Danone and others. The finance, resources, technologies, staff, skills and access to markets that large corporations can bring can be important to social enterprises. Public-interest organisations can therefore look to large corporations as potential partners in helping develop or scale social enterprise. However, in research for this guidebook it was not possible to find examples of large NGOs working with large corporations to develop or scale social enterprises. Instead, there appear to be two largely separate arenas. One the one hand, there are non-profit organisations such as Ashoka.org that work in support of individual social entrepreneurs. On the other hand, there are large firms that seek to engage with social enterprises directly, with the support of consulting groups such as Volans (**Box 10**). This is likely to change in future as general enterprise development has long been a feature of development agency work, and the move to developing social enterprise in concert with large companies does not require a major step forward. In so doing, NGOs and development agencies could learn a lot from the way groups such as Ashoka prioritise the types of people and enterprise to support. Jack Sim of the World Toilet Organisation is keen to point out that 'anyone who has a big bureaucracy and large overheads is probably not a suitable partner for

---

17   www.skollfoundation.org/skollworldforum/index.asp, www.schwabfound.org/
     sf/Events/WorldEconomicForumEvents/2010/index.htm
18   Personal communication, October 2010.

social enterprise projects'.[19] It appears that large NGOs may need to become increasingly nimble to be effective partners in this field.

What can public-interest organisations seek from large companies for development beyond partnership with social enterprises or developing new products for BoP markets? Discussions and initiatives in response to this question have given rise to the popularity of 'inclusive business' as a framework for understanding business contributions to development. The term 'inclusive business' describes the belief that business can have a greater positive impact on development by adapting their core business to encourage development outcomes, rather than through new niche BoP initiatives, corporate philanthropy or support for social enterprises.[20] 'Inclusive business' is defined by the United Nations Development Programme (UNDP) as 'business models that create value by providing products and services to or sourcing from the poor, including the earned income strategies of non-governmental organisations'.[21] The focus is less on small enterprises seeking to address social needs profitably, but rather on large firms being able to adjust their core businesses to benefit more people as consumer, employee or supplier.

The private investment arm of the World Bank, the International Finance Corporation (IFC), has begun promoting inclusive business models.[22] Their research with Harvard University identifies some important lessons for people who want to engage companies to do more 'inclusive business'. They found that most companies that engage in more inclusive business practices do not do it for reputation, risk management or innovation promotion. Those traditional drivers of voluntary responsibility are not sufficient to make a real difference to investment strategy. Instead there has to be an obvious model for sales growth for companies to invest significantly in including more people in the sphere of their positive impact. The research also does not find any success from specialist base of the pyramid (BoP)

19 Personal communication, October 2010.
20 Caroline Ashley, 'Harnessing Core Business for Development Impact' (Background Note; Overseas Development Institute, February 2009; www.odi.org.uk/resources/download/2714.pdf).
21 UNDP, 'Creating Value For All: Growing Inclusive Markets' (2008; www.undp.org/gimlaunch).
22 Beth Jenkins, Eriko Ishikawa, Alexis Geaneotes and John Paul, 'Scaling Up Inclusive Business: Advancing the Knowledge and Action Agenda' (Washington, DC: International Finance Corporation and the CSR Initiative at the Harvard Kennedy School, 2010; www.ifc.org/ifcext/advisoryservices.nsf/AttachmentsByTitle/BOP_Scaling_Up_Inclusive_Business/$FILE/BOP_Scaling_Up_Inclusive_Business.pdf): 36.

approaches, but a 'whole pyramid approach'. Beth Jenkins and her co-authors explain that:

> most of the commercially viable, scalable examples . . . take more of a 'whole pyramid' approach in which the poor are segments within a much broader overall market, supplier base, or distribution network . . . Cemar, for example, was required by law to electrify the entire state of Maranhão in Brazil's low-income northeast region. The company was permitted to charge higher-income, higher-usage customers higher tariffs – enabling it to cross-subsidize those with low requirements and abilities to pay, with the government providing additional subsidies. In the telecommunications cases, the companies started in markets at the top of the pyramid to develop steady revenue streams and recoup their infrastructure investments, which eventually put them in a position to develop products and distribution channels for lower-income clients, with lower average revenues per user . . . [The findings] may signal that new or more nuanced thinking is warranted on some of the assumptions that have become generally accepted knowledge in the inclusive business space – for instance, that doing business with the world's [poor] will require radical innovations in technology and business models.[23]

This analysis leads to a key conclusion, which is the essential role of governments in creating enabling conditions and even imperatives for inclusive business. One of the most successful examples in the IFC study is from the Philippines, and the often highly charged issue of private provision of water services. The IFC highlighted how the Manila Water Company is effectively providing water for impoverished communities due to the company and the government planning to ensure the successful meeting of public need and private expectations. Through a series of partnerships between the company, municipal governments and local communities, low-income neighbourhoods not only have access to water but are themselves central to the efficiency and cost savings components of Manila Water's inclusive business model. Metering systems were developed to ensure ease of monitoring and transparency and, where such systems were not practical, usually in very poor communities, bulk metering and cost-sharing programmes were introduced which permitted self-monitoring through collective responsibility. The community is engaged to maintain the system and administer collections, which directly supports local employment, generating a local interest in the entire scheme, including on-time payment, and discouraging water theft. The resulting benefit to the community is superior service and water

---

23 *Ibid.*

quality while actively participating in keeping the costs of water low.[24] In many countries the private provision of water by large corporations has created criticism and even protest. In Manila an important means of ensuring that costs have been kept down is that the government required Manila Water, as part of their licensing deal, to cross-subsidise so that they charge wealthier consumers more in order to fund the infrastructure for poorer consumers. This suggests an important role for government in encouraging some forms of inclusive business, including through regulations that require inclusive practices in return for licences.[25] A crucial implication of this finding for public-interest organisations is that partnering with business does not mean that governments become less relevant, or that regulations become less relevant. Rather, government policies may be key to the success or failure of effective business partnerships for development. Therefore when engaging companies it is important to keep public policy on the agenda, and for public policy lobbying to be a potential activity of a partnership.

The IFC research found a general lack of good examples of inclusive business by large firms. 'Large-scale success stories – reaching large numbers of poor people directly or via replication – are still the exception, not the rule,' conclude Beth Jenkins and her co-authors.[26] Given that the companies in the IFC investment portfolio are receiving funds from a development-oriented institution, one might assume some examples of inclusive business, yet only about 100 were found to have a potential inclusive business dimension, in addition to about 100 micro-finance initiatives. That is roughly 13% of the IFC investment portfolio.[27]

Many people working in the inclusive business arena, whether in NGOs, government agencies or business, have called for greater collaboration to create enabling conditions for more inclusive business. For this purpose, the IFC has called for more collective action on issues such as the dual evaluation of business activities, the development of in-depth market information on the needs, aspirations, capabilities and limitations of low-income consumers and producers, as well as on awareness-raising, education and training for low-income consumers, suppliers, distributors and retailers. In a

24 *Ibid.*
25 Ximena Mora Lopez, 'Promoting Inclusive Business: Seeking Opportunity in Crisis' (Asian Development Bank, 2009; www.adb.org/Documents/Events/2009/Poverty-Social-Development/promoting-inclusive-business-Derksen-Lopez-paper.pdf).
26 Jenkins *et al.*, 'Scaling Up Inclusive Business'.
27 IFC funded 1,579 companies in 2009. IFC, *Annual Portfolio Performance Review – FY09* (IFC/R2009-0227; 25 August 2009): 14.

seminar on this topic co-hosted by IFC and Harvard University, participants described a need for 'greater transparency [from potential donors to inclusive business projects] about what is possible and on what terms; faster decision-making and execution; and more judicious, strategic communication with external parties and the public at large.'[28] Therefore donors and other public-interest organisations now need to be clearer about what kinds of project are worthy of support and what management systems need to be in place to promote success. Some donors have measurement systems, such as the IFC's own 'development outcome tracking system'; however, such systems do not yet include the social and environmental standards that are already agreed by the wider international community as important aspects of sustainable development. Other goals, such as the MDGs, and standards, such as the ILO conventions, were not designed for business directly, while the UNGC only provides generic principles that are not comprehensive (not including health, for instance). Attempts to make broad goals such as the MDGs relevant to companies by using them as the basis for measurement tools, as with the MDG scan, are useful for bringing attention to core business contributions to development, but they do not assess the full impact of business. For instance, the data on employment creation does not distinguish between a decent job and forced labour. Standards such as the ISO 26000 social responsibility standard, which was agreed in 2010, may prove useful, but as it focuses mostly on reducing negative impacts of business practice, it will not be sufficient for guiding inclusive business and social enterprise, where the intention is to generate positive impacts in specific ways.

Therefore a more holistic and integrated approach to business contributions to development and their measurement is required – a form of sustainable, inclusive business. The field of inclusive business is important enough now for new management tools to be developed to ensure good practice. To begin with it is necessary for public-interest organisations and progressive companies to define the personal qualities of managers (**Box 25**) and the characteristics of business projects (**Box 26**) that enable beneficial engagements by large enterprises in low-income communities.[29] I offer these qualities and characteristics to seek in potential business partners, as guides for NGOs, development agencies and donors working in the inclusive business

---

28 HKS, 'Starting and Scaling Inclusive Business Models: Summary of a Dialogue', co-hosted by IFC and the CSR Initiative at the Harvard Kennedy School, Washington, DC, 9 April 2010: 3.

29 *Ibid.*

field. By enhancing clarity on what kind of business projects and partners are suitable for sustainable development and using these as guidelines for partnering, public-interest organisations may avoid some of the pitfalls of partnering outlined in the previous chapter.

Box 25 **The sought-after qualities of managers of sustainable, inclusive business**

Key personal qualities that are important for business executives in large corporations to move their organisation towards helping poverty reduction in a sustainable way:

1 **Active**. Aspiring to be a conscious agent of sustainable development in ways that involve core business

2 **Coherent**. Addressing both the positive and negative impacts on low-income communities of current and planned business activities, leaving no issue ignored for long

3 **Self-aware**. Focusing on your new USP – your 'Unique Serving Points' – by identifying the special capabilities you bring to a particular situation

4 **Transformative**. Seeking enterprise opportunities that disrupt obstacles to social progress

5 **Creative**. Using methods and indicators that promote creative teamworking to innovate new solutions

6 **Inquiring**. Learning together with unusual colleagues, sharing your own approaches while appreciating low-income communities and their organisations as co-innovators, while increasing your understanding of the complexity of development issues (including by applying the project characteristics; Box 26)

Box 26 **Project characteristics of sustainable, inclusive business initiatives**

A particular business project should have the following characteristics in order make a positive contribution to sustainable development:

1 Provides products, services or decent work to lower-income communities in ways that stimulate more sustainable production and consumption patterns as a whole

2 If outcompeting goods and services produced by locally owned operations, then offers superior eco-social qualities to existing options, and provides local employment

3 Supports a mixed-ownership economy

4 Provides new sources of capital to community members

5 Provides community members with new access to markets, on stable and transparent terms

6 Transfers appropriate technology and skills to community members

7 Generates a return on investment that is acceptable to the company to be part of a scalable business, without future reliance on cash or in-kind subsidy from government or voluntary sector partners

8 Supports good governance and enabling conditions in the local community and nationally, in accordance with relevant UN principles on human rights and development

9 Involves mechanisms for participatory monitoring, evaluation and learning that address each of the preceding characteristics, to inform future strategy and operations.

Projects that do not exhibit these characteristics may create some benefit, but risk causing new problems in the communities they affect, and therefore may have unintended negative consequences for both sustainable development and the performance and reputation of the organisations involved.

Box 27 **Future guidance**

The following initiatives are providing training or guidance on cross-sector partnering.

The Partnering Initiative at the International Business Leaders Forum

A global hub for learning about partnerships, enabling the sharing of practical experience, contributing to cutting-edge knowledge, offering support, training and advice as well as setting standards in what constitutes good partnering practice.
thepartneringinitiative.org

Partnership Brokers Accreditation Scheme

Established in 2003, this is a professional qualification (the only one of its kind) for those involved in scoping, designing, developing and managing partnerships.
www.partnershipbrokers.org

The Collective Leadership Institute

Founded in 2005 as a non-profit organisation based in Berlin and Cape Town, its mission is to build dialogic process competence for cross-sector sustainability engagement. It offers educational programmes, project management, process-oriented research and networking.
www.collectiveleadership.com

Engaging Change Programme

A work programme of Lifeworth Consulting, to enable participatory evaluation and strategic planning processes for organisations seeking to promote system change through their cross-sector partnering. This guidebook is the second publication of this programme, following up the special issue of *Business Strategy and the Environment*, called 'Beyond Partnerism'.
www.lifeworth.com/consult

Emerging Leaders Innovate Across Sectors (ELIAS)

A global innovation and learning community that focuses on regional platforms for facilitating multi-stakeholder innovation across entire systems. Coming together around specific thematic and geographic concerns, participants from government, business and civil society embark on a shared sensing and innovation journey in order to deepen their understanding of their current systems and to discover and prototype new ideas and collaborative opportunities that could transform the system.
www.presencing.com/capacitybuilding/elias.shtml

iScale – Scaling Impact

A network of organisations and people that develops, promotes, applies and shares innovations for scaling impact in addressing global challenges. It recognises that a broad range of stakeholders in government, private sector and civil society are creatively working to address these problems together and seeks to provide them with tools to scale their impact. In particular it advises on effective multi-stakeholder network management.
www.scalingimpact.net

The UN Global Compact LEAD Transformative Partnerships Project

A project of the UN Global Compact with leading business members, to advance the development of new transformational cross-sector partnerships that address the systemic causes of public problems. This research and dialogue platform provides advice to UN agencies and business partners on the characteristics and challenges of the third generation of partnering.
www.unglobalcompact.org/HowToParticipate/Lead/index.html

Conclusions

The universe is transformation;
our life is what our thoughts make it.

Marcus Aurelius

As societal partnerships have proliferated, a body of experience of what works and what does not has developed, some of which is documented, some not. Criticisms of the limitations of partnerships have grown, often shaped by a perception that they are championed by powerful organisations to avoid deeper and faster changes to their practices, such as those that come from changes in public policy. Therefore, some public-interest organisations are turning away from partnerships, while others continue to collaborate with business but grow concerned about partnership progress. To the latter, the cross-sector relations that have been created appear too important to let go, but the issue remains about how best to harness those relations for their organisation's mission. This guidebook offers support, to improve their proficiency in partnering, and to reassess their approaches to partnering to ensure their existing relations are contributing to, and not hindering, wider and faster changes towards their missions.

Initially some organisations and individuals have reacted defensively to criticisms of partnerships. However, if organisational learning is a key benefit from partnering then we must strive to be better learners. It is important to avoid the 'group-think' that may result when people seek a consensus to maintain their projects and partnerships. To fully engage critique, as valid feedback, is an essential part of learning. A prerequisite for learning is to be prepared to risk our own security, such as our current world-view and financial status. If we are attached to an easy life, and seek reassuring mental and material patterns, we may only learn more sophisticated self-justifications, a form of solipsism that is the exact opposite of the idea of inquiring together. Alternatively, if we continue to engage openly with an ever-widening circle of interest and opinion then we may become part of a connective wisdom on how the human race might transcend our current social and environmental challenges.

The evolution of partnering has required that feedback is critical in order to learn and adapt. One of the most recent insights from evolutionary science on the useful role of viruses provides a helpful metaphor. When mapping the human genome, researchers discovered that 8% of our genome is composed of broken and disabled retroviruses which, millions of years ago, embedded themselves in the DNA of our ancestors. Some scientists argue that, without these retroviruses embedding in this way, mammals might never have developed a placenta, which protects the foetus and gives it time to mature. That provides an evolutionary advantage over birds, reptiles and fish, as eggs cannot eliminate waste or draw in the maternal nutrients required to develop the large brains that make mammals versatile. 'It is quite possible that, without [retroviruses embedding themselves in DNA] human beings would still be laying eggs,' explains one scientist. The fact that humans are partly descended from viruses may be surprising, but reminds us that things which attack us can sometimes make us and our descendants stronger. Similarly, the substance of, and the information contained in, a critique can be incorporated into the routines of an organisation, in ways that strengthen it.[1] Although it is increasingly popular for executives to speak of 'embedding this in our DNA', no organism has been able to embed DNA in its own DNA – but a virus can. To apply the metaphor appropriately would mean executives inviting attack in order to incorporate the DNA of the critique into their organisation's own DNA. The experience with the evolution of partnerships suggests that would not be such a strange idea.

As professionals we all face daily challenges in working together to deliver results that serve greater goals, rather than dealing with the near-term needs of our own team or department, and our organisation's bureaucratic routines. To serve the common good, all of us do well to remember that just

---

1   For more on this science, see: www.newyorker.com/
    reporting/2007/12/03/071203fa_fact_specter?currentPage=all.

because we work on a matter of public concern does not mean we work for the public benefit. Just because we always thought we were doing good, does not mean that we do so today. Just because we proved our commitment in our activist days does not mean we are moral agents today in our new roles. We must no longer simply hope that we are having some effect or hope that something useful might come of our work in business, finance or public policy. Instead, we must make our judgement now, and live with the consequences. Whether something we do is good or bad depends not only on the act itself, but on our intention and the context of our act. It is not simply what we do, but what love we bring to doing it, that matters. If we act with loving compassion for humanity and nature, and therefore subsume our self-interest to that wider scene, then the right course of action in any professional situation will become clear.

To keep a focus on the greater good effectively requires a form of awareness, consciousness even. The three generations of partnering described in this guidebook reflect the different mindsets of some of the participants in the partnerships. Each involves an ability to recognise ever broader sets of relations that impact on the issues and organisations involved.

- First-generation partnerships involve 'doing something different'. They do not challenge one's normal assumptions, beliefs or behaviours, but involve doing something additional

- Second-generation partnerships involve 'being something different'. They involve a questioning of how one normally operates, and seeking to behave in a better way

- Third-generation partnerships involve 'becoming something different'. They involve recognising that one's behaviour is not solely determined by one's own choices, and that support is needed from others in order to become continually better

Once you have worked through the exercises in this guidebook, either on your own or with colleagues, then you will be better prepared for the next step in engaging business for greater social change. The next step is to begin more wide-ranging and creative conversations with current and potential corporate partners. You may find such conversations are aided by escaping your respective office environments and exploring ideas on neutral and natural ground. You could seek facilitation of creative processes by professionals who are experienced in helping shape collaborative innovation. You could also hone your powers of persuasion by reading one of the numerous communications advice books in the management section of bookstores. There will be many ways to improve your implementation, once you have identified your general goals and strategy, which is what I have sought to help you with in this guidebook.

During implementation of the third generation of partnerships the many challenges that I've outlined in Chapter 6 call for conscious management. Thousands of years ago Phaedrus remarked: 'an alliance with a powerful person is never safe'. As true today, participants in transformative partnerships will need to guard against co-optation. In particular, people working in organisations that play a role in setting standards or advising on them need to understand the potential conflicts of interest when involving companies, and how they can have serious consequences, as highlighted by the cases of WHO and FAO in Chapter 6.

In general, public-interest organisations will need greater clarity on how they view the relationship of corporate power to their particular organisational mission, and the values from which that mission arises. Previous analysis of the approaches of NGOs to corporations revealed four key views on corporate power. For some, corporate power presents an **opportunity**, if it can be directed to better use. For others, corporate power presents an **obstacle**, a problem in a specific case because it was being used in ways that hinder their particular social or environmental objective. With both of these perspectives, people are not inclined to speak or think of corporate power as one phenomenon, as they see the power as being different depending on the corporation in question. Others develop a wider and more categorical critique of corporate power, considering that it is an **obstruction**, a general systemic problem arising because of the logic of capital accumulation driven by stock markets, which leads to externalising costs, and shaping discourse in ways that hinder social and environmental objectives. A fourth attitude to corporate power can be identified, where it is regarded as an **obscenity**. Such people consider it morally wrong for corporations to have their power no matter how it is used, because they consider human self-determination, freedom and democracy to be fundamental and therefore the most powerful institutions in society should be democratic, or controlled via democratic means, as a matter of principle.[2]

Paradoxically, some people in public-interest organisations who are engaged in third-generation partnerships see corporate power as all four of

---

2   Bendell, *Barricades and Boardrooms*: 19.

these Os, at the same time. They see corporate power as an opportunity, yet know that ultimately it must be reduced, through re-embedding it in new social frameworks. It requires a remarkable level of awareness and commitment for business leaders to share that view, and use their power to support new ways of holding their own institutions accountable. That is a form of societal leadership, at the top of the responsible enterprise strategy pyramid, which demonstrates a 'radical corporate citizenship'. That is citizenship in its real sense – seeking membership of a political community, to which rights and freedoms are relinquished, in return for benefiting from the fact that others must do the same. Therefore, in the absence of an international framework of mandatory obligations of corporations to society, real corporate citizenship involves supporting the development of such a framework, in return for the right to international ownership and movement of capital assets. The accountability of those frameworks to peoples of the world will be crucial. New institutions of collaborative governance that involve business, government and civil society should not lead to the sidelining of the goal of collective self-determination that is at the heart of democratic traditions.[3]

As the forms of partnerships I describe in this guidebook obtain greater influence, the people who participate in and manage them will need a mindset for dealing positively with the complexities involved. An awareness of the importance of individual mindsets will also grow through the experience of third-generation partnerships in trying to effect system change. Some will come to understand that influencing personal consciousness is a key way to affect the way people engage in the infinite number of processes and systems they connect with day by day. Consequently we may eventually see a fourth generation of partnering that combines the universal with the personal, to raise the consciousness of people within and influenced by the partnership. In such a situation the inner world of partnering will have become more important.

All of us hold myths and stories in our minds to make sense of existence and experience. Evolution is a powerful story in contemporary society. Evolutionary science does not suggest that we are genetically hindered from an integrated consideration of the 'me', 'we' and 'all of us' dimensions to our lives. Rather, such an integral awareness might be the fittest form. A full 150

---

3 This concept of radical corporate citizenship and the implications for global governance was developed in the conclusion of Jem Bendell, *Terms for Endearment* (Sheffield, UK: Greenleaf Publishing, 2000; www.greenleaf-publishing.com/ngo).

years after the concept of evolution became popular through the publication of *On the Origin of Species*, it is time for us to reconsider the perspectives on human life that evolutionary science can inspire. Unlike Darwin's subtitle to that famous work, which spoke of 'the preservation of favoured races in the struggle for life', contemporary evolutionary science emphasises that cooperation with and contribution to populations and ecosystems are as important to success as individual competition. I have adapted these insights to provide a framework for understanding and evaluating changes in partnering forms and performance.

However, this work is not a science: the most important factor in making partnerships an effective tool for social change is the people who use them. We need more people who are prepared to work on solutions that address the true scale, urgency and depth of the challenges. As leading management thinker and consultant Peter Senge writes: 'The changes in which we will be called upon to participate in the future will be both deeply personal and inherently systemic.'[4] The same place from which we suffer with our knowledge of the state of the world is source of the solution. That place is interconnectedness. The challenge now is to work on those interconnections – to be at once both deeply personal and highly systemic.

---

4   Peter Senge, C. Otto Scharmer, Joseph Jaworski and Betty Sue Flowers, *Presence: Human Purpose and the Field of the Future* (Cambridge, MA: Society for Organizational Learning, 2004).

Box 28 **List of exercises**

Title	Exercise	Box	Page
Understanding partnerships	A	3	16
Inspi(RED) fund-raising or (REDwash? The case of Product(RED)	B	6	31
Assessing your generation of partnerships	C	11	56
Reflecting on a company's readiness to partner	D	12	62
Assessing your organisational stage of targeting the market	E	13	65
Mapping readiness to partner	F	14	66
Partnership SWOT	G	16	72
Developing a plan for evaluating partner fitness	H	17	79
Evolving to the second generation	I	19	87
Beginning a journey to third-generation societal partnerships	J	21	98
Clarifying a desired transformation and transformational partnership	K	22	100

About the author

Jem Bendell PhD

Associate Professor Jem Bendell is an adviser, educator, researcher and writer with 15 years at the forefront of innovations in business responses to sustainable development.

With a PhD in international policy, over 100 publications (including four books and four United Nations reports), Dr Bendell is an award-winning international authority on business–society relations, lecturing in 15 countries and quoted in media such as *The Financial Times, International Herald Tribune, El País, Tatler* and on CNBC.

Since graduating from the University of Cambridge, Bendell has sought collaboration with people who seek to contribute to, and benefit from, the transformation of markets to promote global well-being.

Director of Lifeworth Consulting, coordinating a team of 16 associates, Dr Bendell works with UN agencies, international charities, universities and business, in over a dozen countries, having lived and worked in eight. He has helped create innovative initiatives, including the Marine Stewardship Council, to endorse sustainable fisheries; the Financial Innovation Lab, to promote sustainable finance; founded and runs CSR Geneva, a network of over 700 professionals in Geneva; and the Authentic Luxury Network, for professionals promoting responsible luxury goods and services.

As an academic, Dr Bendell has lectured at business and design schools around the world, has worked with the dean of a business school in Australia to make it a leading sustainability school in the Asia Pacific, and has been an academic convener for three international conferences on this subject (in the UK, Switzerland and Australia).

His personal blog attracts over 30,000 individual visitors and his company's portal of jobs and events in corporate responsibility averages 8,000 visitors each month.

Bendell's current focus is the potential of luxury brands, international finance, management education and inter-organisational collaboration to promote a movement towards global well-being. His 'Deeper Luxury' report on the responsibility of luxury brands appeared in over 50 newspapers and magazines worldwide in the month of its release and continues to appear in fashion and business press today. Bendell's fourth book, *The Corporate Responsibility Movement*, was published in 2009. His next book, *Higher Ends: Sustainable Luxury Management and Design*, is published in February 2011.

Lifeworth Consulting

This guidebook was prepared by Lifeworth Consulting. It is a boutique consulting firm that inspires and connects people and organisations, innovating ideas, strategies and projects, so you succeed by contributing to a fair and sustainable society. Founder Dr Jem Bendell explains the approach:

> We improve the social and environmental effectiveness of people and organisations. Key to real progress is relating changes at individual, organisational, sectoral and societal levels. At Lifeworth we do that by enabling and motivating professionals to improve in concert with changes in their operating environment and society. Whether you work in the non-profit, business or public sectors, we have knowledge, processes and networks to help, having worked in each sector ourselves. So we take a network approach to improving organisations, sectors, policies and societies; and as a network of independents, our low overheads and flexibility mean we offer cost-effective teams tailored to the specific needs of a project. Consequently we only work with people seeking social innovations for transformative change, who benefit from our assets and approach.

Our 18 associates are experienced in working with different cultural contexts and sectors, as well as on a variety of responsible enterprise or societal challenges. We are located in Chennai, Geneva, Grenoble, London, Madrid, Manila, Rotterdam, Toronto and Washington. Between us we speak eight languages including English, French, German, Italian and Spanish. We each have particular crafts that we maintain excellence in, to provide for our clients, in addition to specialist knowledge in responsible enterprise. All our associates are involved in responsible enterprise because of a passion to transform economic life to make it more affirming of life as a whole. Lifeworth Consulting's services include strategy, creativity, communications, liaison and education.

Strategy

Rapidly changing environments mean leaders require strategies that seek shared organisational and societal value. We bring insight from different sectors and cultures as well as social, political and technological trends and concepts to inform strategic planning or enhancement. We focus on both opportunity and risk.

We have advised on strategy development for FTSE 100 companies, working closely at board or senior level, and managing stakeholder engagement in the process. We advise on the delivery of such strategies including policy development, integration between international operations, performance benchmarking, establishment of targets and key performance indicators, stakeholder relations, and the selection of evaluation and audit regimes and suppliers. Areas include brand development, carbon management and responsible supply chain management.

We have advised public and voluntary organisations on their strategies, policies and programmes for influencing or engaging with business. We can produce methodologically advanced reports to inform strategy.

Our intellectual contribution to this field of practice includes the book *The Corporate Responsibility Movement*, which describes the emergence and importance of applying 'movement thinking' in effectively planning responsible enterprise efforts.

Creativity

To successfully respond to the social and environmental challenges faced today requires not only an appreciation of risk, but a creative outlook that sees the new opportunities to create solutions. This requires a passion for change, and constant exposure to different cultures and contexts, which we bring to our work on inspiring socially and environmentally positive creativity. Such creativity can occur within any business function, and inform or enact strategy.

We have inspired creativity in some of the world's leading international organisations, helping them innovate new responsible enterprise and finance initiatives. We have also conceived ideas for clients which have led to the creation of successful new organisations.

Our intellectual contribution to this field of practice includes a keynote speech at the *International Herald Tribune* luxury industry conference, which encouraged an emotional commitment to sustainability that will unleash sustainable design innovations.

Communications

To be part of a solution to social and environmental challenges requires that those whom you depend on for your success join you on the journey. Leaders must therefore influence whole value chains, sectors and even systems of economic, social and political activity.

We have helped clients communicate their responsible enterprise efforts through managing annual sustainability reporting cycles and writing annual sustainability reports (from concept to final publication), including two award-winning sustainability reports for multinational FTSE clients, and related web content.

We have helped clients by conceiving, creating and executing sustainability-related campaigns to generate millions of dollars of editorial press coverage for an outlay of less than £40,000.

We write books, UN reports, magazine and newspaper articles, popular blogs and academic pieces, and make keynote speeches, which generate significant media coverage worldwide and are influential in our field. We publish an annual review of responsible enterprise that is well read by relevant professions. We can also leverage the two professional social networks we have founded and the 4,000 members of our jobs bulletin on responsible enterprise.

Our intellectual contribution to this field of practice includes the report *Tipping Frames*, which explains how the responsible enterprise field is a place for the reconceptualising of cognitive frames shaping society and business, and how to use that for positive outcomes.

Liaison

Different organisations in different sectors – public, private and civic – have different competencies and networks that can be combined to deliver change at the scale and pace that is required by today's challenges. To do this effectively requires advice from those who understand each sector and know when and how partnerships can succeed or fail, and act as a trusted interlocutor.

We have connected international NGOs to create new organisations, UN agencies to environmental NGOs to launch a fashion show, sovereign wealth funds to responsible finance initiatives, and helped business schools, companies and sovereign wealth funds to join UN, NGO or multi-enterprise initiatives. We develop stakeholder engagement programmes, from the head office of UK-based FTSE 100 client, to a site-level stakeholder relations plan for a gold mine in West Africa.

We have created two successful professional networks that provide the opportunity for people to connect. CSRGeneva.org and AuthenticLuxury.net each convene around 700 members in active online communities that also meet regularly.

Our intellectual contribution to this field of practice includes *Partners In Time?* which was the first UN report on business–NGO partnerships for sustainable development.

Education

The past decades of management education have encouraged specialisms that do not help us to see the whole system of an organisation, value chain, sector or society. To navigate the rapid changes in environment, society, economics, politics and technology, executives can benefit from experiential, transdisciplinary, heart-felt and practical education, which also provides them with new contacts and ideas.

We developed and teach master's-level education for responsible enterprise at universities in Australia, Singapore, Switzerland and the UK. We have developed and delivered intensive sustainability training courses, for companies in Spain and Sweden, for instance. We have run workshops at corporate responsibility conferences around the world.

We are currently developing a network of social and environmental entrepreneurs, who are willing to host study tours of their premises, in order to offer this as part of our educational programmes.

Our intellectual contribution to this field of practice includes commentary on business education and research in a quarterly column in the *Journal of Corporate Citizenship*.

More information is available at www.lifeworth.com/consult